THE BIG BOOK OF

AMAZING NAMES

GYLES BRANDRETH

ILLUSTRATED BY JANE ANDREWS

CORGI BOOKS

THE BIG BOOK OF AMAZING NAMES

A CORGI BOOK 0 552 542717

First published in Great Britain by Corgi Books Ltd.

PRINTING HISTORY
Corgi edition published 1985

Corgi Books are published by Transworld Publishers Ltd.,
Century House, 61-63 Uxbridge Road, Ealing, London
W5 5SA.

Made and printed in Great Britain by the
Guernsey Press Co. Ltd., Guernsey, Channel Islands.

First Names
Surnames
House Names
Nicknames
Place-names
Pet Names
Pen Names
Stage Names
Fun Names

from Adam and Eve to Zero Zzyzz,

they're all in

THE BIG BOOK OF AMAZING NAMES

This book is for
Saethryd
a very special girl
with a very special name

Other books by Gyles Brandreth

CONTENTS

Introduction 7

A Africa, Asia, America, Australia and
  Antarctica 8
B Botticelli 11
C Columbia Old and New 15
D Dunroamin 19
E Ecuador Equals Equator 24
F Fido and Friends 29
G Guess Who? 36
H Hannah and hannaH 40
I Indiana Jones and Company 43
J Janus, Mars and Augustus 48
K King Dick 54
L Limerick Lines 58
M Master Molloy Molony 62
N New Names for Old 66
O Ohm, Watt and Bell 72
P Plummer & Leek (Plumbers) 77
Q Quisling and Others 81
R Royal Progress 85
S Secret Meanings 89
T Terry and Teresa, Thomas and Thomasina 95
U Underwood and Wodehouse 101
V Vera Rave 107
W Wellington's Boots 111
X Xavier and Other Saints 115
Y Y, France 120
Z Zero Zzyzz 123

INTRODUCTION

It's hard to avoid names. Whatever we do or wherever we go they surround us. Our parents, our friends, towns, streets – even the budgie – they all have names. And so, of course, do you: though if you don't like yours, you might find some ideas in the book for a new one!

For some tribes in the world, a person's true name is so important and secret that only close relatives are allowed to know it. Everyone is normally called by a nickname. This is to stop magicians casting evil spells that use names on people. Sounds silly? Maybe, but until recently in Britain it was thought that a baby's name should be kept a secret until it was baptised. This was to stop the Devil gaining control of the young child.

So names are important, but they are also fun! You can have hours of amusement simply making up silly names for people, and this book will give you some ideas. You'll also discover how names came about and why there's a person who delights in the surname – Zzzzzzzzz! You'll travel around the world, finding out where Kicking-Horse Pass is and learn the name of the world's first re-usable spacecraft.

Welcome to the wonderful world of names!

AFRICA, ASIA, AMERICA, AUSTRALIA AND ANTARCTICA

Welcome to the wonderful world of names. The world is full of amazing facts, and that includes facts about names. Did you realise, for example, that five of the six continents in the world, Africa, Asia, America, Australia and Antarctica, all begin and end with the same letter – 'a'? The other continent, Europe, also starts and ends with the same letter – in this case, 'e'. Read on and you'll discover the world's most popular name, America's cuddliest president and much, much more. . . .

The longest place-name in the world is: **Krungthep Mahanakhon Bovorn Ratanakosin Mahintharayutthaya Mahadilokpop Noparatratchathani Burirom Udomratchanivetmahasathan Amornpiman Avatarnsathit Sakkathattiyavisnukarmprasit** . . . better known as Bangkok, capital city of Thailand! The official name of the city is, fortunately, simply **Krungthep Mahanakhon**.

Britain's longest place-name is: **Llanfairpwllgwyngyllgogerychwyrndrobwllllantysiliogogogoch** – a small railway station in Wales.

As many as 100 million people in the world bear the surname **Chang**, which makes it the most-used name on Earth. The most common first name is **Muhammad**.

The nineteenth-century French conductor **Louis Jullien** had 36 first names, each one coming from one of his 36 godparents.

William Shakespeare, the English playwright, spelled his surname in at least eleven different ways.

The person with the longest-ever name in Britain was **Major L. S. D. O. F. Tollemache-Tollemache-de Orellana-Plantagenet-Tollemache-Tollemache**, who died in 1917.

Until the seventeenth century, most children were only baptised with one first name in England.

There are eight towns with the name of **Rome** in the United States.

Theodore Roosevelt (1858–1919), once President of the United States, gave his name to the cuddly toy animals we know as 'Teddy bears'.

A man belonging to the Maya Indians has three different names in his life. The first is given at birth, the second when he reaches adulthood and his third and formal name is only won when he gets married.

BOTTICELLI

Names and games were made for each other. Some name games, like inventing silly names, you can make up as you go along. Others, like the ones below, have a few rules – though you can change them if you want to. Let's look first at the well-known word game called **Botticelli**.

Botticelli

Any number can play this game, which is named after the fifteenth-century Italian painter, **Sandro Botticelli**. It could have been named after any famous person, for the idea of the game is to guess the identity of a well-known figure, chosen by one of the players. This player can think of any famous person – real or from a book – but it should be someone the other players know about.

The other players are told only the **first** letter of the person's surname, perhaps 'B'. They then take it in turns to ask **indirect** questions about the identity of the person, such as '*Are you a famous children's author?*' The questioner **must** have a particular famous person in mind – for example, here it could be Enid Blyton.

The first player might reply, '*No, I am not Enid Blyton,*' or,

11

'*No, I am not J.M. Barrie*.' But if he can't think of a children's author whose name begins with 'B', then the questioner is allowed to ask a **direct** question. This is to get more information, and could be something like '*Are you living?*' or '*Are you British?*' To this question, the first player must answer, truthfully, '*Yes*' or '*No*'.

The first player might be forced to reveal the mystery person either by a direct question, or by an indirect one. For example, suppose the hidden name is Ludwig van Beethoven. A player might ask '*Are you Beethoven?*', which is obviously a direct question. Or he might ask, '*Are you a nineteenth-century German composer who wrote nine symphonies and went deaf?*' – the answer would be the same! Whoever asks the question which reveals the person gets to choose someone for the next round.

Famous Names

One player reads out a list of surnames of famous people. The other players (any number over three can play) have to write down as many of the first names as they can remember in two minutes. Two points are given for each correct name, one for the correct initial. The player with the most points wins.

I Love My Love

The players should sit in a circle. They take turns to start the game by saying, '*I love my love with an "A" because he/she is . . .*' Here the player thinks of a suitable word, which must begin with an 'A', for example, '*adorable*' or '*athletic*'. They then continue by saying, '*He/she is . . . (name beginning with 'A', like Ann or Andrew) and he/she lives in . . . (place-name starting with 'A', such as Africa or Ambridge)*'. The next person in line has to repeat the same words, this time using the letter

'B', the third person with the letter 'C' and so on. If you can't think of a name or adjective or place beginning with your letter then you go out. The last person remaining is the winner.

Step Forward

Here's a game to play out of doors or in a large room. The players line up facing one player who acts as caller. The caller calls out a letter. If one of the players has this letter in their name, they take a step forward. If they have this letter in their name twice, they take two steps forward, and so on. The first person to reach the caller wins. To make it more fun the caller should say the letters quite quickly, and if a player takes a step by mistake he should be made to go back two paces.

Initial Answers

This is a game suitable for three or more players. One player is chosen to be questioner. He or she asks each of the other players in turn the same question – for example, '*What food do you like?*' Each player must reply with a phrase which has the same initial letters as his own name. So to the question, '*What food do you like*' Frank Sinatra might reply, '*fried sausages,*' and Sebastian Coe might suggest, '*sponge cake.*' If a player can't think of a food that matches his initials then it's his turn to ask the questions.

Car Games

You probably already know lots of games to play during car journeys. One game using names is where players score points for each name they see which contains, for example, a type of tree. So '*Oakfield Road*' would win a point, as would the town '*Ashford*'. You needn't stick to trees – the game works as well with animals or plants. The player who collects the most points wins the game.

Name Fame

There is no limit to the number who can play this game. Someone suggests the full name of a well-known figure. The other players then have to think of a suitable phrase to describe that person, using words that have the same initial letters as the person. For Florence Nightingale you could choose '*friendly nurse*'. In the case of William Shakespeare, '*witty scribbler*' might be suitable, or you could describe the cricketer Geoff Boycott with '*great batsman*'.

COLUMBIA OLD AND NEW

Give something a name and you feel much closer to it. People have long given names to pets, houses, mountains, boats, and now aeroplanes and spacecraft. Here are some famous or unusual craft to have been given names, beginning with a well-known name in the United States.

In a continent that was discovered by a man called Columbus the name **Columbia** is a very important one. So it's not surprising that the United States should choose it for a very special spaceship – the Space Shuttle. On April 12th, 1981, *Columbia* took off from the United States, went into space and flew round the Earth 37 times. But the special thing about the Shuttle was what happened next. It returned to the United States and landed like an aeroplane! This made *Columbia* the world's first ever re-usable spacecraft.

There are other American vessels which have had the same name. In 1792 a little steamship discovered a great river on the northwest coast of America. Despite being so small this little boat gave its name to the mighty waterway – the river *Columbia*. And did you know that the spacecraft flying round the moon when Neil Armstrong stepped out onto the moon was also called *Columbia?*

Even that's not the full story. A 102-tonne yacht named *Columbia* won the American Cup sailing race for the Americans in 1899, beating the British yacht *Shamrock*. It also beat the British yacht *Shamrock II* in 1901 – though at first the Americans didn't think she was good enough to be in the race! Yachts called *Columbia* have also won the cup in 1971 and 1958.

Apart from playing bowls and defeating the Spanish Armada (with some help, of course!) Francis Drake also had time to sail around the world in his little boat *The Golden Hind*. In fact, when Drake left Plymouth harbour on his journey on December 13th, 1577, his ship was called the *Pelican*. It was not until he reached the Straits of Magellan, a passage of sea at the tip of South America, that Drake renamed the ship *The Golden Hind*. The name comes from the symbol on the crest of Sir Christopher Hatton, an important man who gave Drake money to pay for the voyage.

Science has helped to design and build many ships. However, it is science that owes a great deal to one ship, *HMS Beagle*. It was aboard this ship that the great scientist **Charles Darwin** sailed on 27th December, 1831, on his famous voyage. For five years Darwin collected information about different plant and animal species. He used this knowledge to help write a book called *The Origin of Species*, published in 1859, that rocked the world with its suggestion that Man has descended from apes and not from Adam and Eve.

Could you believe that the largest ship in the world, weighing over 46,000 tonnes, and over 250 metres in length, could hit an iceberg and sink within three hours – on its first voyage? This is what happened in 1912 on April 14th to the liner *The Titanic* which got its name from the giant Titan. The tragedy was headline news all over the world. Only 700 of the 2,200 passengers survived – amazingly there were only enough lifeboats for about half of the people on board!

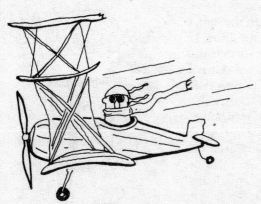

Aircraft too have been given names. Here are a couple of the most famous ones. No prizes for guessing which would win in a race!

Orville and Wilbur Wright were the first men to fly in an aeroplane with an engine . . . but what was the plane called? Many think it was the *Kitty Hawk* but actually the plane was called *Flyer!* The first flight was on December 17th, 1903.

The world's fastest airliner, the *Concorde*, first flew in 1969 on March 2nd. Its first passenger service was on 21st January, 1976. In 1975, *Concorde* became the first aircraft in the world to make two return transatlantic crossings in one twenty-four hour period – that meant crossing the Atlantic four times! Why is the plane called *Concorde?* The idea for the aircraft was a joint one between Britain and France, and the French word for 'agreement' is, yes, '*concorde*'.

Man reached an historic point on October 4th, 1957. For the first time a man-made object, the satellite *Sputnik 1*, was sent into space to orbit the Earth. This was only 54 years after man had managed powered flight for the first time.

Russians must regard the name *Vostok 1* with special affection. For it was in this craft that the Russian cosmonaut Yuri Gagarin became the first person ever to leave the planet. Fortunately, he returned two hours later! The flight took place on April 12th, 1961. Soon afterwards, on May 5th, the first American in space, John Shepard, made his voyage.

DUNROAMIN

Having a name for a house is much more attractive than simply giving it a number. House names can also tell you something about the person who lives in the house. And have you ever thought what the name of your house means? You may be surprised. Take the common example of the name **Dunroamin** (or **Dunromin**). It may sound Scottish but in fact the name is short for '*I've done roaming*'. People who have retired from the Army or Navy quite often use this name. **Dunhuntin, Dunmoovin** and **Dunlukin** are other names used in the same way. Can you think of any more that could begin with Dun? **Duntrekkin**, perhaps?

There are other ways that houseowners can describe their final home. For example, **Stayinholm, Settledown, Gone to Ground** and **Rest-a-Whyle**; though the owner of the last place doesn't sound quite settled yet! Not so the person who named **Jusrite**, who seems to have found his ideal home. Some people seem to go to a great deal of trouble to find the right home. So we get house names like **Hardearned** and **Ardwun**. Maybe buying **The Struggle** took a lot of effort and perhaps a **Copper Coin** was all the owners had left after buying their house!

Common House Names

One of the most common names for a house is **Belle Vue**, which means good or fine view in French. Even more common nowadays is the Italian expression **Bella Vista**, while some householders use the Spanish words **Buena Vista**, which also mean the same. **Sea View** is a name used in many English seaside towns, though the newer **What-a-View** is much more interesting.

Houses called **The White House** may simply be describing the colour of their walls. On the other hand the owners may be people who consider themselves important . . . for The White House is the home of the President of the United States! Would anyone dare to call their house Buckingham Palace?

One very common name for a house is **Avalon**, the '*Land of the Blessed*' where King Arthur is supposed to be buried. **Lancelot** and **Guinevere** are also used as house names, but strangely few houses are named after Arthur himself, though **Merlin**, the name of Arthur's magician, is widely used.

You've probably seen the name **Chez Nous** used for someone's house. This is the French for '*at our place*' or '*at home*'. Less common but still used is **Chez Foux** – but beware of the people living here because it's the French for '*The Home of the Mad People*'!

Hillcrest describes a house on the top of a hill, but can you guess what **Alcrest** means? It's not the name for a house that covers 'all' of a hill – instead it's short for **A**fter **L**abour **C**omes **R**est! The owners are obviously putting their feet up after a hard life!

In the Doghouse

Although the English are very fond of animals not many houses are named after pets in this country. There is, however, one place called **Poodleville**, and **Beagle** and **The Cat House** are sometimes used. More unusual, and very clever, is the name **Dalsida**, the home of a **Dal**matian, a **Si**amese and a Great **Da**ne! Oddly, fish provide a few names such as **Trout Hollow, Minnows** and **Dolphin Cottage** as well as the wonderfully named **Oyster Haven**. Much more common are houses which take their names from different types of fruit such as **Appleyard, Plum Tree House, Peach Cottage** and the unusual **Chez Bilberry**. Some 'nutty' names include **Walnut House** and **Almonds**. Other kinds of food rarely give their names to houses, which is a pity when you consider how delightful **Muffins** and **Christmas Pie House** sound!

The list of houses that have got their names from the world of nature, the weather and the animal kingdom is almost endless. Here are just a few examples:

Greenacres	**Little Clouds**
Fieldside	**Badgers' Hollow**
Peppercorns	**Deer Leap**
Windwhistle	**The Squirrels**
Sunshine House	**Toad's Green**

Famous Names

Giving a house the name of a famous person can make it

sound quite important. For instance, there is a **Newton House** in honour of the famous scientist, and a **Mozart** named after the great eighteenth-century composer Wolfgang Amadeus Mozart. Royalty is also popular, and **Kingswood** and **Queenswood** are quite common, as well as **Baronsmead** and **Ladyswood**. Some good names come from characters in books or poems, such as **Lorna Doone** or **Hiawatha**. But surely the best name of this sort belongs to a house named after Sir Arthur Conan Doyle's most famous character: **Sherlock's Holme!**

Could you spell that please?

When people start using foreign names for houses the postman's problems begin. Fortunately no one sends many letters these days to **Ekal Zag. Du. Nu. Tuk. A**, for this ancient palace has disappeared! Its name means '*The Palace Without a Rival*'. But imagine trying to spell these names correctly:

Warrawee – 'come here' in the language of the Australian aborigine
Shanthi Gruha – 'peaceful home' in Hindi
Kalyan Kutir – 'good luck' in Gujerati
Kuan-Yin – Chinese
Longhen-E-Yeigh – 'pond of the geese' in Manx
Tarroo-Ushty – 'mythological water bull' in Manx
Chy-an-Dour – 'a house by the water' in Cornish

In India there's a place called **Ankh Michuli**, which means '*blind man's buff*' – it was called this because the great emperor Akbar used to play this game there with his harem ladies!

Homesick

When people move from one area or country to another they often like to keep something that will remind them of their old place – and what better than a house name? One way of doing this is to reverse the spelling of the place you come from to make a new word. So, people from Canada can use **Adanac**, travellers from Cornwall would use **Llawnroc**, and homeowners from Wales might call their home **Selaw**. Sometimes housenames are simply the first names of their owners reversed, like **Evilo** or **Revilo**.

House Humour

A lot of house owners have a sense of humour, it seems. How else to explain **Round the Bend, Rusty Railings** or **Crumbledown?** One owner lived next door to a house called **Costa Brava**, after the Spanish coastal area. He decided to call his house **Costa Fortune** – he must have paid a lot of money for it! There are plenty of modern-sounding names around now, such as **Med-O-View, Hi-Jinx, Sudden-Lee, Y Wurree, Fortitoo** (number 42) and **Idunno. Tivuli** doesn't look very exciting until you reverse it to give '*I luv it*'. Some houses give fair warning of the type of person you might find in them – **Crazy-dale** and **Nutter's Nest** for example. One house, **Gorldly Woods**, is a spoonerism (that's where the first letters of two words are swapped) of '*worldly goods*', while one place has the ridiculous name of **Shilly Chalet** – '*shilly shally*'! You may not trust the owner of **Bodgers** to do any repair work at **Danpach**, but one of the best house names must be that of a house standing opposite a cemetery – it was called **Spooks!**

ECUADOR EQUALS EQUATOR

You may have been abroad and travelled to different places with exciting names. Or you may have looked through an atlas and seen the great number of country and place-names in the world. But have you ever sat down and wondered why these places have the names they do? What do their names mean? In this section we look at these questions and explain the origins of the names of some well-known – and not so well-known – places.

No one knows for sure where the name of **Africa**, the second largest continent in the world, comes from, but it was probably the name of a single tribe. When the Romans captured the city of Carthage in the second century BC they named the province around it *Africa*, after the Afridi tribe who lived there. Afridi comes from the Arabic *afira* 'to be dusty'. This is not surprising when you consider that this area is now the country we call Tunisia – most of which is covered in desert sand.

Ecuador is a small country at the top of South America. It was so named because the Equator, the imaginary line that runs around the middle of the world, goes through the country. 'Ecuador' is the Spanish word for 'equator'.

The reason for **Evening Island's** charming name is quite simple – it was discovered by Carteret in 1767 at sunset. The island is also called Lord North Island.

The strange thing about **Greenland** is that it is mostly covered with snow and ice – hardly what you'd expect of a country with such a name! Greenland was so called by the Viking, Eric the Red, who landed there in 982. Although the land was cold and difficult to live in even then, Eric called it 'Greenland' to encourage people to settle there.

If you look at the national flag of **Japan** you'll probably be able to guess what the word 'Japan' originally meant. The flag shows the red beams of a rising sun, and the Chinese name for Japan was *Zhi-pan-kwe* (or *Jih-pan-kwe*) which means '*Kingdom of the Sun Rise*'. The Portuguese version of the word was *Japao*, which became Japan in English.

One unfortunate traveller has good reason to remember **Kicking-Horse Pass** in the Rocky Mountains of the United States. Sir James Hector, an English geologist, was crossing a river in the mountains when his horse became upset and kicked the unlucky Hector in the chest – which laid him up for several days. The story of the incident led to the naming of the river 'Kicking-Horse River', and soon the nearby pass took its name.

Unlike most countries, **Liberia**, a small West African republic, has a very definite and fixed beginning. In 1822 a group of Americans created a settlement in West Africa for those slaves in America who had become free citizens. From this settlement a state was set up – its name, Liberia, means '*land of the free*', a very suitable name for the first independent republic in West Africa.

Melbourne is the attractive capital city of the state of **Victoria** in Australia. It is one of the few large towns in the world to be named after a British Prime Minister, Lord Melbourne. This happened in 1837, the year Queen Victoria came to the throne – she, of course, gave her name to the state Victoria. Remarkably, at least five other places were named after her: the capital of British Columbia, in Canada; a lake in East Africa; waterfalls on the river Zambezi; an island in the Arctic and land in the Antarctic.

Unlike some other places **Mistaken Point** was not named by mistake. It is called Mistaken Point because sailors sailing along the coast of Newfoundland are liáble to mistake this piece of land for Cape Race, which is further to the east. It must give them a shock if they seem to sail by the same part twice!

Montevideo is the capital of Uruguay, in South America. Its name had an odd beginning. In 1520 the Portuguese explorer Ferdinand Magellan was exploring the coast of South America. He and his men travelled for many kilometres over very flat land, when suddenly a young sailor saw a hill 230 metres high and was so surprised that he called out *'monte vejo!'* – I see a mountain! This was written down and later the area became known as Montevideo.

The land of cowboy hats and oilwells, **Texas** only got its name because of a mistake. Originally, a tribe called the Assinaes lived in this area. In 1690 a Spanish monk called Father Damian came ashore in the region. He asked the tribesmen what their name was and he got the reply *'texia'*. Father Damian assumed this was their tribal name and called them *'Tejas'* – in fact, the word meant *'good friend'*!

TEJAS!

Poor Christopher Columbus was a great sailor, but when he found islands to the West in 1492, he was rather confused. He thought Haiti was Japan, Cuba was China and Costa Rica was Malacca! This led him to call the new islands the **West Indies** to go with the 'East Indies' Vasco da Gama had discovered. Despite this great mistake, the name has remained ever since.

One of the newest country names in Africa, **Zimbabwe** used to be called Rhodesia, after the explorer Cecil Rhodes who governed the country. The new name comes from the name of a remarkable ruined city. It was made of stone – Zimbabwe means *'stone houses'* – and was one of the strongest cities ever built in Africa, at a time when most houses were made of wood.

FIDO AND FRIENDS

For many people the names they give to their pets are every bit as important as the names they give to their children. And if pets are supposed to look like their owners, perhaps pet names can tell us what the owners are really like! Here we have a look at some common and interesting names for pets, and then at some real animals in history.

Fido and Friends

One of the most common names for a pet dog is supposed to be **Fido**. The name means 'faithful' in Latin, which makes it a good choice for 'man's best friend'. But like the other common names for dogs, **Rover** and **Towser**, Fido is really not that common any more. Some of the more common names are **Patch, Butch, Shep, Brandy** and **Whisky**, or **Sally, Rosie** and **Tessa** if the dog is female. These seem a little boring compared to some names used in America, which include **Bug-a-Boo, Poojie, Bo-Peep** and **Dum-Dum**! There was once a famous dog actually called **Rover** who appeared in a play by George Bernard Shaw. If you're looking for a name for a dog here are a few suggestions more interesting than **Spot** or **Jack**. And remember, if you're training a dog it is better to have a short, simple name which can be learned easily and which you can shout quickly if you have to!

Ma Ajmal –	how beautiful!
Roh –	ghost, soul
Saqr –	falcon
Monkey Face –	common name for Afghan Hounds
Zobeedee –	after the favourite wife of Haroun Al Rashid in the *Arabian Nights*

Man's Best Friend

The trust between man and dog has always been very strong. There is a story that Frederick the Great of Prussia (1712–1768) was once saved in battle by his dog **Gengisk**. It seems that the dog rushed onto the battlefield where Frederick was riding. By loud barking Gengisk was able to warn his master of the approaching Russian cavalry. Man and dog rushed to hide under a bridge – not very dignified for a king but at least it was safe!

One brave dog has a town in Wales named after him. The town is Beddgelert, in Snowdonia, and its name means 'grave of Gelert'. **Gelert**, a hound belonging to a Welsh chieftain named Llewellyn, was left to guard Llewellyn's baby son while his master was out hunting. But when the chieftain returned he found the hound covered in blood, the baby's cradle upset and blood-smeared, and no sign of the child. Thinking Gelert had attacked his son, Llewellyn killed him with his sword. But later he found the child unharmed, and lying near him a huge wolf which Gelert had killed while defending his charge. Overcome with remorse, Llewellyn buried his faithful hound in a special grave, and the place came to be called Beddgelert.

Tiddles and Co

Cats are more independent animals than dogs, and are quite often given more interesting names. However there are some very common cats' names still in use. **Tiddles** is one, and **Sandy, Fluffy, Puss, Whiskers, Kitty** and even **Moggy** are widely heard. Names describing colour are extremely popular for cats, for example **Ginger, Snowy, Torty** (for tortoiseshell cats) and even **Satan** (for black cats). Fortunately some owners provide their beloved moggies with more interesting names. One little kitten was called **Woolly Bully**, while another cat had the splendid name **Mr Bojangles**, after a character in a song. Mark Twain, the great American writer, called one of his cats **Zoraster**, after an ancient Persian prophet. Another writer fascinated by cats was the poet T. S. Eliot, whose *Old Possum's Book of Practical Cats* was adapted to create the famous *Cats* musical. The cats in Eliot's book had wonderfully imaginative names: **Skimbleshanks, Bustopher Jones, Mr Mistoffelees, Rumpelteazer**. I wonder how many cats have been named after them?

Here are some more exciting names for cats.

Bella Adorado – adoring and beautiful
Archibald Buchanan – cat named after Archibald meaning 'valiant' and Buchanan who was a President of the United States

| **Bouhaki –** | first cat known to have a name – owned by King Hana in eleventh dynasty Egypt, it sat at the King's feet wearing gold earrings! |
| **Picklepuss –** | same cat also called *Monsieur du Piquel* |

Archy the Budgie

Cats and dogs are not the only pets that deserve names. From the largest elephant to the smallest insect, a pet isn't worth having unless it has a name. For a start you could call a goldfish **Jaws** or **Moby Dick** – though this probably won't keep the cat away! **Archy** is a good name for any bird because this is short for *Archaeopteryx*, which was the very first bird. Or you could call a lizard **T. Rex** after *Tyrannosaurus Rex*, the fierce flesh-eating dinosaur. One great achievement is to be the only person with a pet of a particular name. The person who had a hamster called **Smeagol** must have been the first person to call such an animal by that name, that of a character in J. R. Tolkien's book *The Lord of the Rings*. If you don't find a name suitable for your pet in the following list, don't worry. At least pets can't answer back if they don't like what you call them!

| **Ah Ah Weh –** | American Indian name for a duck |

Blinker –	good name for a frog
Bulls-eye –	Bill Sikes' dog in *Oliver Twist*
Cuthbert –	for a donkey, since its diminutive, Cuddy, is a Scottish name for a donkey
Hajja Ba Ba –	children's name for a real rabbit
Jemima Puddle Duck –	from a story by Beatrix Potter
Kaa –	name of python in *Jungle Book*
Mr Mickey, Peter Pan –	good names for budgerigars
Mustard and **Pepper** –	two Dandie Dinmont terriers in Scott's *Guy Mannering*
Nana –	the Newfoundland dog in *Peter Pan* who was nursemaid to the children
Noah –	for a tortoise as it means 'long-lived'
Poll/Polly –	for a parrot, whose nickname it has been since 1630 although no-one seems to know quite why!
Talbot –	for a dog as a talbot is an extinct type of hound – also a nickname used by Chaucer to mean a dog
Mrs Tiggy Winkle –	hedgehog in a story by Beatrix Potter

| Tutenkhamun – | name given to a goldfish |
| What-A-Mess – | the Afghan puppy in Frank Muir's series of books for children |

Animals in History

When you next see a jumbo jet flying in the sky you can remember that the word **Jumbo** comes from one elephant. This Jumbo was London Zoo's first ever elephant, and he was a big one, standing nearly four metres tall and weighing over six tonnes! Jumbo was bought for a circus by Phineas T. Barnum in 1881, and for several years he was a superstar performer. Sadly, this marvellous animal was killed by a train in 1885, a death that shocked the world. His name lives on, however, as a word for anything that is very large; for example, a jet aircraft.

Horses for Courses

In past times a horse was much more than a pet for a person. Horses were the best means of transport (unless you liked walking!) and were often used in war. Let's take a look at some famous horses and their riders.

The Spanish Knight El Cid ('the Master') was famed for his bravery in battle. No less brave was his horse, **Babeica**, a white horse which was

very strong and fast. Oddly, Babeica means
'fool', for people thought El Cid was wrong to
choose a horse that was weak when it was young.
But even after its master's death the horse was
loyal. The Spanish tied El Cid's dead body to his
horse and sent it charging into battle against the
Moors. The Spanish soldiers were so happy to
see their heroic leader that they managed to beat
the Moors quite easily! In 1948 a monument to
Babeica's memory was built in Spain.

> The jet black horse, **Bucephalus**, belonged to
> one of the most famous soldiers in history
> – Alexander the Great. Alexander rode him in
> every major battle – some say Alexander was
> more concerned with Bucephalus than with his
> own soldiers! Certainly when Bucephalus died
> after being wounded in battle, Alexander was so
> upset he founded and named a city after the
> horse – Bucephala. The horse's name came
> from the shape of a brand mark on its fore-
> head – *Bucephalus* means 'ox-head'.

Copenhagen belonged to the Duke of
Wellington, and carried him through the entire
seventeen-hour Battle of Waterloo. When the
horse eventually died, twenty-one years later,
he was buried with full military honours.

Marengo was Napoleon's famous charger, which he rode
during all his battles in Italy and Austria, and at the Battle of
Waterloo. Marengo's skeleton is kept at the National Army
Museum at Sandhurst in England.

GUESS WHO?

For centuries men and women have sought for signs of whom they would marry. Why not try some of their old customs?

Throwing the Apple Peel

The use of apple peel for predicting the name of one's true love is well-known. First you peel the apple, taking care to keep the peel whole (you can eat the rest of the fruit). Then stand up straight and throw it over your left shoulder. If it breaks it means you have no sweetheart. Otherwise the peel should take the shape of your true love's initials.

Crabbing for Husbands

This custom consists of picking crab apples and arranging them in the shapes of various suitors' initials. The apples are left until Michaelmas Day (September 29th) when the best preserved apples would show the best prospect.

The Dumb Cake

This has nothing to do with how clever you are at cooking. The cake should be made by a single girl, either at Christmas or when she's fasting. While she's baking it she must not speak – that's why it's called a 'dumb' cake. Once the cake is made the girl should carefully carve her initials in the top, and leave the cake by the fireplace. While she is asleep the spirit of her future husband is supposed to come and carve his initials next to hers. Apparently it is very important to leave the front door open for the spirit to pass through. No one knows what would happen if the door was closed, but it could be something bad.

Ball of Primroses

Girls in Wales used to have a very pretty way of finding the names of their sweethearts. They made a little ball out of primroses, or cowslips if they preferred, and threw it up into the air. While they were throwing the ball they recited this little verse:

Tisty, tosty, tell me true
Who shall I be married to?

They then quickly called out a list of people who might be suitable husbands. Whichever name was said at the moment the primrose ball hit the ground was the name of the future partner.

Bible and Key

One more complicated way of finding the name of your future husband or wife is with a Bible and a key. Take an iron door key and put it in the Bible at the Song of Solomon or the Book of Ruth with the key resting on the words '*Let him kiss her with the kisses of his mouth*', and with the ring of the key sticking out at the top. Then bind the Bible with a garter from the right leg (or an elastic band if you don't have a garter) to hold the key in place. Next you should get two people to suspend the Bible by putting their fingers under the ring of the key (you can do it yourself if you want to be secretive). The next part of this custom is to recite the following words from the Book of Solomon:

'*Many waters cannot quench love, neither can the floods drown it. Love is as strong as death, but jealousy is as cruel as the grave, and burneth with a most vehement flame. If a man should give all the substance of his house for love, it would be utterly consumed.*'

When you've done all that you recite the alphabet slowly. The Bible will turn when the initial of the first name is reached. Repeat the alphabet to discover the initial of the surname. If this method is too long for you try the same process but instead of reading from Solomon simply say, '*Bible, Bible tell me true, the name of the man I am to marry*'.

Following the lead . . .

A much simpler method altogether was to use some molten lead. An important day of the year was chosen, for example, Hallowe'en or New Year's Eve, and the lead was poured into a container of cold water. The lead became solid and formed the initials of the future spouse. This custom is not recommended nowadays, however, for it is difficult and dangerous to melt lead.

Herbs in the Fire

This is a form of *pyromancy*, that is, telling the future by use of fire. First collect some suitable herbs – for this sort of 'magic' **catnip, rose petals** and **bay leaves** are the best. Throw these onto a fire and say some appropriate words – these must rhyme. You might say, for example:

*'When the fire settles down
Make my future partner known.'*

That rhyme is good enough but magic is a very personal affair so it's probably better to make up your own words. It's best to throw on the herbs in an evening and return to the fire the next day. There, in the undisturbed ashes, you will see the name of your future husband or wife. One more point, you must use this method on a Friday, the day of love and romance, otherwise you'll have burnt the herbs for nothing.

Snail Magic!

Surely the strangest way of finding the name of your true love is by using a snail. Get up early on May Day, before the sun rises. Go for a walk outside and find a snail and then take it back to the house. Sprinkle some flour on an old board (some say you should use a kitchen table but it's no fun sharing breakfast with a snail) and put the snail on it. Leave the snail for an hour or so. When you return the snail will have 'written' the initials of the person who loves you best, or the person you'll marry. If nothing has been written leave the snail for another hour, but it could mean you'll marry late in life. If after the second time the snail still hasn't written anything it's time to stop – or get a new snail!

A similar custom is to put a snail caught on Hallowe'en Day in the ashes of a fire and let it trace the initials in the same way, but make sure it's not too hot for the poor snail.

HANNAh AND hANNAH

Hannah is a special name. If you turn it round and spell it backwards you get . . . yes, **Hannah**. Words like this, that are spelt the same backwards and forwards are called *palindromes*. The longest palindrome in the English language is **redivider**, though there is also **rotavator** which is a trade mark.

Names, too, can be palindromes – Hannah is the best example but other names include:

Ada	**Eve**
Anna	**Odo** (seventeenth-century name)
Bob	**Pip**

Can you think of any more?

The surname of at least one twentieth-century politician was a palindrome – Pierre **Laval** (1883–1945), a Frenchman who came to an unfortunate end when he was executed for treason for being too friendly with the Germans in the Second World War. One long palindromic name is **Malayalam**, which is the name of the language spoken by the Malayali in the South Indian state of Kerala. But most of the fun to be had with palindromes comes from palindromic sentences. Some people have spent years creating sentences that read both ways and there are a large number of them. Here are some, all containing names.

Madam, I'm Adam.
Delia sailed, Eva waved, Elias ailed.
Did Dean aid Diana? Ed did.
Did I draw Della too tall, Edward? I did?
Draw, O Caesar, erase a coward.
Evade me, Dave.
Max, I stay away at six am.
Naomi, did I moan?
Noel, let's egg Estelle on.
'Not New York,' Roy went on.
Now, Ned, I am a maiden won.
Was it Eliot's toilet I saw?
No mists reign at Tangier, St Simon!
Sums are not set as a test on Erasmus.
Lear's in Israel.
Revenge my baby, Meg? Never!
Sir, I'm Iris.
Sh! Tom sees moths.
Stella won no wallets.
Too far, Edna, we wander afoot.

Do-It-Yourself

You'll have probably noticed that certain names are very useful to the palindromist – words like **Enid** and **Edna**, which when reversed give **dine** and **and** + **e**. If you want to try your own palindromic sentence, it's best to take a name, like **Mat**, which produces **Tam** when turned around. Then leave a space in between the words like so:

Mat   **Tam**

The next step is to find a word that will join these two up. Here you could simply add 'sees' to get your very own palindromic sentence:

Mat sees Tam.

This is a simple example. Longer palindromes are very difficult to make and can take a long time. But if you want to have a go, good luck!

INDIANA JONES AND COMPANY

If you've seen the film *Raiders of the Lost Ark*, you may be puzzled by one thing: the name of the hero, Indiana Jones. 'Jones', of course, is common enough but 'Indiana' . . .? This, in fact, is the name of one of the states of the U.S.A. Not perhaps the sort of name many parents would give their child, but at least it's better than calling someone 'New York' or 'New Mexico', two other American states.

Although Johns and Janes, Michaels and Mandys and other well-known first names are still the most popular, some parents choose to give their children very unusual names and do so for a variety of reasons.

Best Names First

In the seventeenth century the Puritans were a group of people who believed in living simple, pure lives. They looked down on such pleasures as drinking alcohol, playing games and going to the theatre and chose names for their children to suit their beliefs! Only a very few of these names survive today:

Be-thankful
Discipline
Faint-not
Fight-the-good-fight-of-
    faith
Hate-evil
Help-on-high
Humble
Kill-sin

Meek
Peaceable
Reformation

Search-the-scriptures
Sin-deny
The-Lord-is-near
Truth
Weep-not

Precious Jewel

Quite often the unusual name given to a child is a word that already has a well-known meaning. For example, with the names **Spring** and **Autumn** – the children were probably named after the season in which they were born. But why **Pebbles?** Was this child found lying on the beach? Or maybe her father was an **Admiral**, who found the baby while at **Anchor** (both first names). Valuable stones and metals are to be found as names, the parents hoping that the magic of these jewels will rub off on to their **Precious** children – for example **Diamond, Ruby, Sapphire** and **Silver**. Some parents obviously want names to help their little ones to grow up as nice boys and girls. So we get **Butter**, who wouldn't melt in the mouth of little **Angel**, while **Smart** young **Princess** is likely always to have **Gladness** in her heart – especially if she finds a good **Friend!**

Nature, in all its glory, can provide some unusual names. On a day when you have **Sunshine** you may come across a beautiful **Blossom** as you walk around. With **Elderberry** trees around you and a **Raven** flying overhead you might chance to look out at the **Ocean**, and if you're lucky you might see a **Dolphin** – unless it's too **Dark!** Interested by these names? Then run like a **Gazelle** to your parents, be **Meek** (call your father **Sir**), tell them you're a **Star** and ask for a **Lucky** name that will give you more **Glory!**

Believe it or not, **all** the above names have been used in real life!

Novel Names

Writers are fond of making up odd names for the people in their books. Some, like **Jheral** and **Tinzy**, are unlikely to catch on, but a few names have. In this list you can see where the names were first used:

Kimball – From Rudyard Kipling's story *Kim*.

Lorna – From R.D. Blackmore's *Lorna Doone*.

Mycroft – The name of Sherlock Holmes' brother.

Rhett – Rhett Butler was the hero in the famous book and film *Gone With the Wind*.

Robinson – From Daniel Defoe's character Robinson Crusoe.

Wendy – Was first used by J.M. Barrie in *Peter Pan* in 1904. It was originally a pet name used by Barrie for

W.E. Henley's small daughter, Margaret. She was called 'Friendy' which became 'friendy-wendy' and eventually just 'Wendy'.

Finding a name that very few other folk have is not too difficult – if you want you can make up your own. Try spelling a common name backwards. Jim will give you **Mij**, while Mike comes out as **Ekim** – and you can be sure not many have those names! But if you're still stuck for ideas then here's a list of real first names that are fairly unusual – at the moment:

Girls

Alanjil	Larenda
Alvetta	Leetra
Aminatta	Lichelle
Audette	Marnita
BG	Mellyn
Bonzetta	Quansetta
Brochelle	Retina
Buffy	Samona
Cappucine	Shalette
Charnel	Shemika
Clavandra	Shey
Daneen	Starmania
Darsha	Tanzia
Diresa	Tavis
Elonda	Tempest

Fadwa
Frechette
Harolynn
Hiawatha
Ietta
Jakarta
Janella
Julanda
Kale
Kozara

Turila
Ulyssia
Vana
Versia
Vilisha
Vonda
Wyvetta
Yoshette
Zella

Boys

Arrow
Bonus
Coma
Emit
Esquire
Fateful
Free
Friar
Handy
Heron
Ichabod
Income
Inez

Khaki
Major
Murder
Only
Pickles
Rice
Sarepta
Senior
Sory
Thistle
Treasure
True
Worthy

JANUS, MARS AND AUGUSTUS

Months of the Year

Nowadays we're used to the idea of a year divided up into twelve months, with each month having a certain number of days. Let's take a look at how these months and days got their names.

The first month of our year is **January**. Janus was an important Roman god, in fact so important that when they prayed, Romans always called upon Janus first, even before the great god Jupiter. An image or carving of Janus was often put over a doorway, with his face looking outside and inside at the same time – the Latin for doorway is *ianua*. No one knows for sure if Janus took his name from the doorway or the doorway took its name from this mighty god. But we do know that the Romans called the first month *Januarius*, because it was the 'entrance' to the year, and this was how we got the word January. And of course, when January comes we look both ways as well – we think of all we're going to do in the next year . . . and all we wish we hadn't done in the last!

The Latin word for **February** was *Februarius*. At this time of year the Romans had a festival called *februa*, which was a time of making things pure (from the word *februare*). One of the customs was for people to walk through the streets carrying lighted candles. Later this practice was followed by the Church. Mothers who had had children in the last year took candles with them as they walked to church. As a result this feast day, on February 2nd, became known as Candlemas Day.

March is another month that takes its name from a Roman god. Mars is best known to people as a god of war, but at the beginning he was a god of vegetation or plants. So the Romans named the month *Martius* to mark the time of year when new life and vegetation starts to grow.

As you will see all the names of our months came from the language used by the Romans, Latin. *Aprilis* was what the Romans called **April**, though no one is quite sure why. Perhaps the most likely reason is that it comes from the word *aperire*, which means 'to open', for Spring is the time of year when leaves and flower buds begin to open.

May was known as *Maius* in Latin, which may have come from a little-known goddess called Maia. However, some people think the name comes from the word *maiores*, meaning 'elders'. But the main reason for thinking this is only that June may have been the month of young people (see below), and so to make it fair the 'old' people were given a month as well!

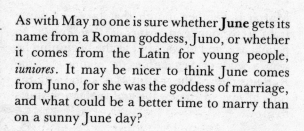

As with May no one is sure whether **June** gets its name from a Roman goddess, Juno, or whether it comes from the Latin for young people, *iuniores*. It may be nicer to think June comes from Juno, for she was the goddess of marriage, and what could be a better time to marry than on a sunny June day?

There is little doubt that **July** took its name from the great Roman Julius Caesar, who was born in July, probably in 100 B.C. As a general Caesar was very successful and he won many battles against the Britons and the Gauls (who lived in what we now call France). He was also the most powerful man in Rome, but he was killed by Romans, including his old friend, Brutus, who feared that Caesar might misuse his power.

August was named in honour of the first Roman emperor, Augustus Caesar who was originally called Gaius Octavius. Augustus became emperor after the death of Julius Caesar. Before August got its present name the Romans called it *Sextilis*, which means the sixth, for there were once two fewer months than there are now! August, of course, is now the eighth month in our calendar.

September simply comes from the Latin *septem*, seventh, before two months were added to make it the ninth month. Confusing, isn't it!

Again, **October's** name comes from a time when it was at a different position in the year. *Octo* was the Latin word for eighth, though now, of course, October's the tenth month.

November comes from the Latin *novem*, ninth, the position it once had in the year.

When **December** was the tenth in the year it took its name from the Latin *decem*, tenth.

Days of the Week

We take the names of days for granted, but they too come from the names of old gods or nature. But unlike the months they don't get their names straight from Latin.

The Old English word for **Sunday** was *Sunnandaeg*, which means 'Sun's day'. The

51

Romans called it *Dies Solis*, which means the same. The Sun is so important to Man that it's natural to have a day of the week named after it.

You can probably guess that **Monday** means 'moon's day', from the Old English, *Monandaeg*.

The Romans called **Tuesday** *Dies Martis*, after their god of war, Mars. The god of war in Britain at that time was called Tiw, or Tyr in Norse. So this day was called *Tiwesdaeg* in Old English. Tyr was supposed to be the son of Odin and was the bravest of the gods. He even lost a hand in defending the other gods and himself. This was when a giant wolf, Femir, threatened to kill Odin, chief of the gods. The gods tricked the wolf by daring him to break free from chains they had made. Femir agreed to be bound, but only if one of the gods put his hand in Femir's mouth in case it was a trick. Tyr accepted this and put in his hand. When the wolf realised he had been tricked and the chain was unbreakable he bit off Tyr's hand!

Wodin was an Anglo-Saxon god who was the father of Tiw (he was called Odin in Norse). Mercury was the Roman god similar to this and the Latin for **Wednesday** was *Dies Mercurii*, day of Mercury. So the Old English for the day became *Wednesdaeg*, which later changed to the present name. Wodin (or Odin) was the wisest god of all. This was because he gave an eye to permit him to drink from a magic stream that gave him wisdom. Sometimes he would walk disguised amongst men, when he was called the Hooded One, the Pleasant One, or sometimes the Terrible One.

In Old English **Thursday** was called *Thuresdaeg*, so named after the god of thunder Thor. Next to Odin he was the most important and powerful god. Thor had a magic hammer that could not be broken and which always returned to him. Once, a giant stole the hammer, and said he would only return the hammer to Thor if he, the giant, could marry the beautiful goddess Freyja. Freyja refused to wed the ugly giant so Thor himself dressed up as the goddess and went to the wedding. Although the giant wondered why his new 'bride' ate so much, he did not suspect that it was really Thor in disguise. The giant agreed to give his bride the magic hammer as a gift, but as soon as he had done so Thor took the hammer, threw off his disguise and killed the giant!

In Latin **Friday** was known as *Dies Veneris*, day of Venus who was goddess of love. The Norse and Anglo-Saxon goddess of love was Frigga or Frigg, and so Friday was called *Frigedaeg* in Old English. According to the Norsemen, Frigga was Odin's wife.

Saturn was the Roman god of agriculture and they named **Saturday** day of the week *Dies Saturni* in his honour. This became translated into the Old English to give *Saeternesdaeg*, which has become Saturday.

KING DICK

Most people at some time in their life get given a nickname, either by family or friends – or enemies. Some, like 'fatty', we can grow out of, but others can last a lifetime. Famous people get their share of nicknames: look at Mrs Margaret Thatcher, nicknamed the 'Iron Lady', or another British Prime Minister, Harold Macmillan, who was known as 'Supermac'! As we shall see kings and queens have been given many nicknames, but we start with a 'king' who wasn't a king at all. . . . Richard Cromwell.

Richard was the son of Oliver Cromwell, a great man who had held England together in troubled times. When Oliver died in 1658, Richard took over as Protector of England, so people called him **King Dick** as he held the most powerful position in the land. But Richard was very weak and fled the country when Charles II returned to become king – and after this people called Richard **'Queen Dick'** because of his softness!

Ethelred the Unready was not a very successful king, but this was not because he was 'not prepared'. For Ethelred's nickname really meant that he lacked 'rede' or good advice. Nowadays we would have called him Ethelred the Ill-Advised!

Here is an example of like father, like son, for **Louis the Fat's** father, Philip I of France, was also very fat. It was said that by the age of 46 Louis, who reigned from 1081 to 1137, was so fat he couldn't ride a horse! There have been many French kings called Louis – nicknames for these include the 'Baboon', the 'Foolish', the 'Universal Spider' and the 'Indolent'.

No one can have earned their nickname more than **Ivan the Terrible** (1530–1584). Thousands died or were tortured under the rule of this fierce Tsar of Russia, and in 1570 at Novgorod his men killed many people, who were thrown into the icy rivers. Finally in 1580, Ivan flew into such a rage that he even killed his own son.

It's not only royalty and rulers who have been given nicknames. An unusual occupation or talent can sometimes lead to a new name being applied. History is full of such cases, as these examples show.

James, Lord of Douglas (1286–1330) was a dashing young man who fought bravely for the Scots against the English. His nickname, **Black Douglas**, comes from a time when he managed to capture Roxburgh Castle – by disguising his men as black oxen!

Baron Manfred von Richthoften became a national hero in Germany during his brief life. He was the greatest air ace of the First World War, though at first he had started the war riding in the German Cavalry. He was called the **Red Baron** because of the all-red Fokker aeroplane he usually flew. He was so respected by his opponents that when he was killed in 1918 he was buried with great honour by the British and Australians.

William Frederick Cody became known as **Buffalo Bill** because he was once a buffalo hunter. At one time he was also a Pony Express rider, and he once beat the great chief Yellow Hand in single combat while a scout for the U.S. army. His fame came from the 'wild west' shows he organised; they contained real cowboys and Indians and in 1887 he brought the show to England with great success.

Lancelot Brown or **Capability Brown** is probably the most famous gardener of all time. In fact he was a landscape gardener, which meant that he designed gardens. Some of his efforts at Blenheim and Kew were very beautiful – and a bit larger than the average garden! His nickname is supposed to come from his habit of saying, '*It has great capabilities,*' when surveying a garden.

A man with the nickname **Soapy Sam** should perhaps have been a laundry man! But Samuel Wilberforce (1805–1873), Bishop of Winchester, won this name for his ability to smooth out opposing views between two people. He joked that the real reason for the name was the way he often got into 'hot water' but came out with clean hands!

If your surname is Martin and you happen to join the navy, chances are that you'll be called **Pincher Martin**. The tradition comes from Admiral Sir William Martin, a very tough man. He was known for putting sailors under arrest – called 'pinching' in the navy at that time – for the smallest reason.

LIMERICK LINES

Limericks are great fun. In case you don't know they are short, usually five-line, poems which tell a short story. Limerick is also a town in Ireland, and some people believe that this form of poetry took its name from that town. Others deny this, but the truth is no one knows for sure where limericks came from. **Edward Lear** (1812–1888) was the first to make limericks popular when he published his amusing *Book of Nonsense* in 1848. In fact Lear has been called the 'poet laureate' of limericks. Like many he became interested in this fun form of poetry by reading this classic limerick:

There was a sick man of Tobago,
Who liv'd long on rice-gruel and sago;
   But at last to his bliss,
   The physician said this –
'To a roast leg of mutton you may go.'

Ouch!

If you want to criticise someone but don't like saying it to their face, then you can let a limerick do your talking. Here Dante Rossetti, an artist, attacks another painter, William Scott:

There was once a painter named Scott
Who seemed to have hair but had not.
   He seemed to have sense:
   'Twas an equal pretence
On the part of the painter named Scott.

But the best bitter limerick must be this one that appeared in *Punch* magazine – the person attacked is the playwright George Bernard Shaw:

There was a young man of Moose Jaw
Who wanted to meet Bernard Shaw;
   When they questioned him, 'Why?'
   He made no reply,
But sharpened an axe and a saw.

Famous Pens

As we have seen many limericks contain names, either of places or of people. Edward Lear made the use of 'Peru', a good rhyming word, quite common in limericks – as this Lear limerick shows:

There was once an Old Man of Peru
Who watched his wife making a stew;
But once, by mistake,
In a stew she did bake
That unfortunate Man of Peru.

Another famous writer who turned his hand to limericks was **Lewis Carroll**. These two examples of his go together:

There was a young man of Oporta,
Who daily got shorter and shorter.
   The reason he said,
   Was the hod on his head,
Which was filled with the heaviest mortar.

His sister, named Lady O' Finner,
Grew constantly thinner and thinner;
    The reason was plain:
    She slept out in the rain,
And was never allowed any dinner.

Limericks Unbound!

The authors of most limericks are never known, and many
limericks are told rather than written down. The limerick is
taken seriously as a poetic form (books have been written on
the subject) but as these examples show the best things about
limericks are their humour and cleverness.

An indolent vicar of Bray
His roses allowed to decay.
    His wife, more alert,
    Bought a powerful squirt,
And said to her spouse, 'Let us spray.'

There was a young man of Calcutta,
Who had an unfortunate stutter.
    'I would like,' he once said,
    'Some b-b-b-bread
    'And also some b-b-b-butter.'

There was a young fellow named Fisher
Who was fishing for fish in a fissure.
  Then a cod with a grin
  Pulled the fisherman in . . .
Now they're fishing the fissure for Fisher.

And finally . . . why not have a go at a limerick yourself? All you need to remember is to make the first line rhyme with the second, the third line rhyme with the fourth and the last line rhyme with the first two lines. Names, which appear in all the limericks above, are very good for 'making' rhymes.

MASTER MOLLOY MOLONY

Pick up a book by **James de la Pluche**. Or one by **Henry Esmond Esq**. Or how about something from **Michael Angelo Titmarsh**? In fact it doesn't really matter which of these you choose for 'all' these people were the same writer: **William Makepeace Thackeray** (1811–1863), the English novelist. Thackeray used many different 'pen names' for his writing, among them the delightful sounding **Master Molloy Molony**. Another good one was **Mulligan of Kilbally-mulligan** – certainly the sort of name that gets you noticed!

Lots of writers have chosen to write under 'pen names' (or *noms de plume* as the French call them) and Thackeray was by no means the first to do so. The great French philosopher and writer **Voltaire** (1694–1778) used more names than Thackeray – in all a staggering 173, including the name Voltaire itself (his real name was François Marie Arouet). But even Voltaire is left behind by the famous author of *Robinson Crusoe*, **Daniel Defoe**, who used at least 198 different names! His real name was Daniel Foe.

One of the reasons writers like Defoe and Voltaire used false names was that they often criticised the government or members of society – both were imprisoned because of things they wrote. So they used different names to try to avoid their real identities becoming known. These days writers are more likely to choose pen names to allow themselves to live a 'normal' life without publicity, under their real name, or to allow them to write different styles of book. We'll begin by looking at what is probably the most famous pen name of all. . . .

Lewis Carroll, the brilliant creator of *Alice's Adventures in Wonderland* and *Through The Looking Glass* was a lecturer in mathematics at Oxford University called Charles Lutwidge Dodgson. He chose his pen name in a rather complicated way by translating his German-sounding name into Latin, and then translating this into English. 'Carroll' and 'Lewis' were the results, and he reversed them to get Lewis Carroll.

Many critics believe that **Joseph Conrad** is one of the greatest ever English novelists, yet at the age of twenty the writer couldn't speak a word of English! Conrad (1857–1924) was an exile who found work in the British merchant shipping service. His Polish name was Josef Teodor Konrad Korzeniowski, which he shortened to Joseph Conrad when he began to write in English, having quickly taught himself the language from newspapers. In 1886 he became a British subject and he took Joseph Conrad as his official name. His best works include *Heart of Darkness* and *Nostromo*.

You are in for a surprise when you hear that the novelist **George Eliot** was in fact a woman called Mary Ann (Marion) Evans (1819–1880). In the nineteenth century it was much harder for a woman to be accepted as an author than it is now, so using a man's name was more convenient for a woman writer.

The writings of the Scottish author **Fiona Macleod** have not achieved great fame, nor are they ever likely to do so. But Fiona Macleod still has a special place in the history of literature. . . . for this was the name of one of the very few men ever to write under a woman's name. The author was William Sharp, and he invented the name Fiona, which was not a name before he used it.

Eric Blair (1903–1950) wanted a more English name: he thought Blair was too 'Scottish' and Eric was too 'Norse'. So he picked on the name of the patron saint of England, **George**, and the name of a river in Suffolk where he had once fished, **Orwell**. There are some stories, however, that the name **George Orwell** was given to him by his publisher. The new name, whatever its origin, was first used for the book *Down and Out in London and Paris* in 1933. His other books include *1984* and *Animal Farm*.

Hector Hugh Monro (1870–1916) wrote many marvellous short stories under the unusual pen name of **Saki**. The mystery of how Monro came to choose Saki as a name, which he first used in

1904, still remains. One theory is that it comes from the old poem called *The Rubaiyat of Omar Khayyam*, which has a line *'And when like her, O Saki, you shall pass.'* Or it could be a shortened version of 'Sakya Muni', a name for the prophet Buddha.

Next to Lewis Carroll, **Mark Twain** must be the most famous pen name of any writer. It's not really surprising that Twain didn't write under his real name, for it was a real mouthful – Samuel Langhorne Clemens (1835–1910). This famous author of *Huckleberry Finn* and *Tom Sawyer* is said to have thought up his pen name from the time he spent on the banks of the Mississippi River. The river pilots would take measurements from their boats to see how deep the water was. Sometimes they would shout, *mark twain!* – 'mark two fathoms', and so Clemens got the idea for his name.

NEW NAMES FOR OLD

Most of us go through life keeping the name that we were born with unless it gets changed by marriage. Americans are fond of using their initials instead of their first names but few people go to the trouble of altering their whole name. But for some folk a change of name may be the key to success. Would Cilla Black have become such a popular entertainer if she had stayed as Priscilla White? Or would Yul Brynner be the famous actor he is if he had not changed his name from Taidse Khan, Jr.? Name changes are most common in showbiz and acting where the sound or look of a name is as important as being able to sing or act. So let's take a look at some of the famous people who have changed their names and their reasons for doing so.

Muhammad Ali is one of the most famous people in the world of sport. Unusually, this champion boxer is also known to people by his original name, Cassius Clay, even though Ali himself never uses it now. Ali changed his name in 1964, the same year that he beat Sonny Liston to become World Heavyweight Boxing Champion. He changed his name because he said Cassius Clay was a slave name given to his ancestors. The new name means 'one who is worthy of praise' – very suitable for a man who is one of the best boxers of all time!

In the world of pop music, **David Bowie** is a very well-known and popular performer. This, however, is not his real name. He was born David Hayward-Jones, and changed it to avoid getting confused with another pop star, David Jones of the 'Monkees'. The new name may have been suggested by the bowie knife, a long hunting weapon that was made popular by the nineteenth-century soldier Colonel Jim Bowie.

Choosing a name is normally a serious affair but pop singer **Elvis Costello** got his new name in a pub! His real name is Declan McManus. The person who suggested the new name was called Jake Riviera, an unusual name in itself. 'Elvis' was chosen out of admiration for rock 'n' roll star Elvis Presley, while 'Costello' was a name used by McManus' father Ross, who was also a singer.

We can be grateful for the tough American actor **Kirk Douglas** changing his name for his original name was a real mouthful – Issur Danielovich Demsky! Douglas chose 'Kirk' because it sounds 'snazzy' – he probably didn't know at the time that it also means 'church'!

Definitely not a pop star! **Genghis Khan** was a ferocious Mongol warrior in the twelfth and thirteenth centuries. 'Temu-jin' was his real name, but in 1206 he called himself 'Genghis', which means 'perfect warrior'. The additional name 'Khan' meant 'lord' or 'prince'.

If you haven't heard of the Hollywood film producer **Samuel Goldwyn** before, then you've missed out on one of the funniest non-comedians ever! He was Polish by birth and went to the United States to live. When he arrived and his Polish name was translated into English . . . it came out as Goldfish! Not surprisingly he wanted to change this, and he became Samuel Goldwyn in 1919. Goldwyn is best known for remarks which don't seem to make sense, but which do mean something in a curious way. Here are some of them:

'Gentlemen, I want you to know that I am not always right, but I am never wrong.'

'I'll give you a definite ''maybe''.'

'Anybody who goes to see a psychiatrist ought to have his head examined.'

'A wide screen just makes a bad film twice as bad.'

You may not have heard of **Haile Selassie**, but you are probably aware of the religion that's named after his original name. The religion is called **Rastafarianism** and Selassie's real name was Ras Tafari Makonnen. Selassie took his name when he became the emperor of Ethiopia, in East Africa, in 1930. The name means 'Power of the Trinity'. Rastafarians, who mostly come from Jamaica in the West Indies, regard Selassie as a god.

Little but lively pop singer **Leo Sayer** started his career as Gerard Hughes Sayer. When he was younger the singer had a great amount of hair, and a friend said, *'He's like a little lion.'* Apparently Sayer liked the idea so much he decided to call himself 'Leo' – which is the Latin word for 'lion'!

In the 1960s **Twiggy** became very famous as a model. She was easily recognised because she was exceptionally thin, even for a fashion model. Her real name is Lesley Hornby, but even at school she was called 'Sticks' because of her thinness. 'Twiggy' was another nickname which quickly became the model's working name.

Pop Names

As we have seen a lot of pop stars have chosen to change their names. Sometimes they change because their old names are too boring, or too long, or too difficult to say. A few get given names which somehow stay with them and a few chose names to specifically fit in with their style of music, like the punk rockers!

See if you can find your favourite singer amongst this list; their real names are given on the right.

Adam Ant	Stewart Goddard
Elkie Brooks	Elaine Bookbinder
Kiki Dee	Pauline Matthews
Bob Dylan	Robert Zimmerman
David Essex	David Cook
Boy George	George O'Dowd
Elton John	Reginald Dwight
Marilyn	Peter Robinson
Gary Numan	Gary Webb
Prince	Prince Rogers Nelson
Johnny Rotten	John Joseph Lydon
Captain Sensible	Raymond Ian Burns
Sting	Gordon Sumner
Poly Styrene	Marion Elliott
Ringo Starr	Richard Starkey
Bonnie Tyler	Gaynor Sullivan
Tina Turner	Annie Mae Bullock

Here are the 'names' of some more well-known entertainers, with their real names to the right.

Woody Allen   Allen Stewart Konigsberg

Michael Caine   Maurice Joseph Micklewhite

Jasper Carrott   Robert Davies

Big Daddy   Shirley Crabtree

Kenny Everett   Maurice Cole

John Wayne   Marion Morrison

OHM, WATT AND BELL

Do you know what Messrs Ohm, Watt and Bell have in common? Apart from being great scientists each has given his name to a unit in science, that is an amount used for measuring something. For instance, metres and centimetres are units used for measuring distance. In this section you'll find out how these and other men of science have given their own names to the English Language as a result of their work.

The **ohm** is the unit used to measure the resistance of a metal to the flow of electricity through it. This is as a result of Ohm's Law, on the subject, suggested in 1843. **George Simon Ohm** who gave his name to the unit was a very clever scientist, but he had one problem – he had very little money. He was forced to write letters to the King of Bavaria asking for help, but it was only after his first book came out that he could live comfortably. Perhaps his greatest reward was to have this unit named after him, though this only happened 39 years after he died, in 1893!

James Watt (1736–1819) was a great inventor and scientist. Today he is best remembered as the inventor of the first effective steam engine (he improved and developed someone else's machine). But his name also appears on countless light bulbs, for he gave his name to the unit used to measure electrical power, the **watt**. Watt came from Scotland, but he eventually set up business with a man from Birmingham called Matthew Boulton. Together they built and developed many of Watt's inventions, including the steam engine. Watt and Boulton were the first to use the term **horsepower** as a unit of power, one **horsepower (hp)** equalling 746 **watts**.

In many ways it is remarkable that **André Marie Ampère** (1775–1836) was able to achieve so much in science and have the **ampère**, the unit of electrical current, named in his honour, for the brilliant French scientist had a deeply unhappy life. During the Reign of Terror in France, when many people were killed for their political views, the young André's father was among those executed. This was such a shock that the boy did not speak for a whole year!

The unit used for measuring light/X-ray/ultra-violet wavelengths is called an **ångström**. It takes its name from the Swedish physicist **Anders Jonas Ångström** (1814–1874). He conducted many original researches and was interested in the Northern Lights (or Aurora Borealis), a curious display of light in the sky in the Northern Hemisphere.

Celsius (or centigrade) is taken for granted as a measurement for how hot or cold it is and many people don't know that there was actually a person called Celsius. His full name was **Anders Celsius** (1701–1744) and like Ångström he was Swedish. In 1742 he simplified the Fahrenheit scale of measurement. But if he was with us today he'd have a shock, for originally he set the freezing point of water at 100°C and its boiling point at 0°C. So if he looked at our ovens today, he'd think they were fridges! Only after his early death were the figures changed round, with boiling point set at 100° **celsius** or **centigrade**.

Everyone knows that **Alexander Graham Bell** was the inventor of the telephone (1847–1922). But he has also given his name to the unit used to measure comparisons of the intensity of sound – the **bel**. We are more aware of the unit **decibel**, which is one tenth of a **bel**. On 10th March 1876, Bell made an historic call to his assistant Thomas Watson. *'Mr Watson, come here, I want you,'* said the great inventor, and the 'Age of the Telephone' had arrived

Gabriel Daniel Fahrenheit (1686–1736) used a thermometer filled with mercury, not the usual alcohol, to develop his famous scale. Although the celsius system' of measurement is more common these days, many people still look first at the **fahrenheit** temperature on the weather forecast to see how hot it's going to be. In Fahrenheit's scale water freezes at 32° and boils at 212°.

Look on the dial of most modern radios and you'll see **kilo hertz**, or its abbreviation **kHz**, written on it. This is a unit used to measure the rate at which the radio waves are moving, that is, their 'frequency'. The **kilo hertz** is simply a larger unit of the **hertz** which is named after the German **Heinrich Rudolf Hertz** (1857–1894). Thanks to Hertz's work, progress was made on the invention of wireless telegraphy.

Of the many achievements of the great **Sir Isaac Newton**, one was to have the unit of gravitational force, the **newton**, named in his honour. Once the famous apple had fallen on his head Newton came up with ideas that explained the world around Man better than anyone else's. Only recently have any of his ideas been changed, though the **newton** is still used. There's also a variety of apple named after him!

In 1919 **Ernest Rutherford** (1871–1937) did something that has changed the course of modern history – he was the first man to split the atom. Atoms are the 'building blocks' of the world, and are so small that they can't be seen with a microscope. Scientists still use the unit **rutherford** to measure the rate at which things happen in atoms.

Napoleon was so impressed with the Italian scientist **Volta's** work that he gave him the title of Count Alessandro Volta (1745–1827). Volta examined and named the unit of 'electromotive force' that is still called the **volt**. His other achievements included inventing the first battery, called a voltaic pile, and making the first hydrogen lamp.

PLUMMER AND LEEK (PLUMBERS)

We've all come across them: people whose names are so well suited to their jobs they seem to have been born for them. **Plummer and Leek** are a good example – what could they be but plumbers? And they really do exist, in Norfolk. Remarkably there is a **Mr Bones** who works as an undertaker in Scotland; there was also once a man called **Sir Edward Pinecoffin**, but fortunately for him he was a government official and not an undertaker.

Here are some more suitably named people:

Cheatham & Steele – Bankers in the United States – would you trust them with your money?

Chief (Clayton) Crook – Police Chief in Ohio, USA. Another 'Crooke', Bernard, is also a Police Chief in the US.

Doctor Doctor – One of many Doctor Doctors: there is also a Dr Bonebreak, Dr Paine, Dr Pang and a Dr Bonesetter who works in India.

Reverend Christian Church – Obviously a holy man, who lives in Italy.

Mr Phang – An oriental dentist in west London.

Dr Gargle – A dentist, now retired, in the US. There was also once a Dr Toothaker, and a Dr Pull still works as a dentist! Dr Boring doesn't sound much better, nor does Dr E.Z. Filler!

Groaner Digger – Undertaker in Texas. It seems there is also a Quick Park Funeral Home . . . useful if someone's dying to see it.

I. C. Shivers – Works as an iceman!

Justin Tune – Chorister. This lad's obviously got a big future in music.

Major Minor – This Major in the US could get confused about himself.

Mr Rabbit – Works for a company called William Hare Ltd.

Mr Shock – Watch out for this man – he works for East Midland Electricity!

Mrs Screech – Singing teacher in Canada.

Commander Sink – An unfortunate name for someone in the United States Navy! Let's hope they give him a desk job.

Lawless & Lynch – Name of a firm of lawyers.

Sam Sparks – Fire Chief.

Mr Vroom – Motorcycle dealer in South Africa.

Names don't have to fit in with someone's work to be funny. **Aristotle Tottle** had an odd name, especially for a pirate! Sadly his name didn't help him to succeed and he was described as a 'very timid, feeble pirate'. **Sir Cloudesley Shovel** was more successful as an Admiral in the Navy. But on his last voyage he managed to run his fleet onto some rocks near the Isles of Scilly. Two thousand men drowned and the Admiral himself was killed by a peasant woman who stole his emerald ring as he struggled ashore! The **Reverend Fountain Wetmore Rainwater** had a remarkable character as well as name. On Sundays he used to sprint to church, read one verse from the Bible, and sprint back again – presumably to keep out of the rain.

A lumber dealer called **Humperdink Fangboner** and a nurse called **Fanny Fangboner** both lived in the same town in Ohio in the United States. Quite a remarkable town by the sound of it, for people named **Ovid Futch, Xenophon Hassenpflug** and **Kitty Ditty** lived there as well! Not everyone is born to succeed: when the oddly named Italian **Hannibal Toto** was asked to fire a salute at a wedding he agreed. Alas, when he fired his shotgun he wounded the groom and twelve of the guests!

Meet **Larry Derryberry**; there's also a **Harry Derryberry** and even a **Jerry Derryberry**. None of them are related to each other so there must be at least three sets of parents with a sense of humour. There's a man who has been arrested by police 890 times and convicted 421 times, which must be a record . . . and his name happens to be **Mr Vice**. And pop star David Bowie obviously wanted his son to attract some attention, for he called him **Zowie**!

Believe it or not, these are the actual names of real people. Enjoy them!

A. Moron
Asa Miner
Bambina Broccoli
Cigar Stubbs
Constant Agony
C. Sharp Minor
Demetrius Plick
Eucalyptus Yoho
Evan Keel
Fang W. Wang
Fishy Step
Freeze Quick
Fuller Zest
Gaston J. Feeblebunny
Grecian T. Snooze
Gretel von Garlic
Halloween Buggage
Miss Horsey de Horsey
Hogjaw Twaddle
Ima Hogg
I.O. Silver
Katz Meow
Kuhl Brieze
Luscious Pea

Major Quaintance
Marmalade P. Vestible
Memory Lane
Moon Unit Zappa and
Dweedle Zappa
Never Fail
Noel T. Tweet
Norman Icenoggle
O. Hell
Oofty Goofty Bowman
Original Bug
Oscar Asparagus
Miss Pinkey Dickey Dukes
Pleasant Kid
Preserved Fish, Jr.
Rapid Integration
Roosevelt Cabbagestalk
Dr Safety First
Sandwich Drinker
Savage Nettles
T. Hee
Ure A. Pigg
Verbal Funderburk
Zoda Viola Klontz Gazola

QUISLING AND OTHERS

Vidkun Quisling (1887–1945) is one of those special people in history who have given their name to a word in the English language, though for him this was no cause for rejoicing. Quisling was a Norwegian politician who betrayed his country to the Germans in the Second World War, and became the most hated man in Norway. For several years he was the head of the government under the Germans, but when the war ended in 1945 he was arrested. So angry were the Norwegians with this traitor that when he was found guilty of treason he was executed. Few mourned his death and **quisling** came to be used to mean anyone who was a traitor.

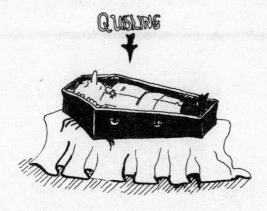

There are a number of other people who because of their strange, brilliant, unusual or just plain daft behaviour have donated their names to our language. So if you want your name to last forever, just follow the example of these great characters. . . .

If you're **barmy** then you're stupid or weak-minded. This word probably comes from **St Bartholemew**, a saint who was harshly whipped. He can be seen in pictures looking rather feeble after the whipping, and so he may have been the first 'barmy' person. One other possibility is that the word comes from a home for mad people that once existed at a place called Barming in Kent.

A **chauvinist** is someone who believes in his country, or his ideas, so much so that he won't accept any other point of view. The poor man who gave his name to this word was a Frenchman called **Nicholas Chauvin** who was a soldier under Napoleon Bonaparte. Chauvin was a devoted supporter of Napoleon, so much so that even the other loyal troops of the general laughed at him. He suffered many injuries but never stopped supporting Napoleon and his name came to mean any person who is almost absurdly loyal to one thing.

Believe it or not **codswallop**, used for anything which doesn't make sense, comes from a real person, **Hiram Codd**. Were he alive today he would probably be most upset at the meaning of the word. In the nineteenth century Codd designed a bottle that closed by having a marble in its neck – the fizzy drink inside would keep the marble in place. 'Wallop' was slang for 'beer' (some people still use the word), the drink often put in such a bottle. Perhaps this clever idea didn't work too well, but anyway this sort of bottle (a codswallop) gradually came to have its modern meaning – most unfairly to Codd!

The word **dunce** nowadays means someone who is stupid or slow to learn. But the first 'dunces' weren't stupid – they just didn't like new ideas! **John Duns Scotus** (1256–1308) was a Scottish priest and important religious thinker. He and his followers, sometimes called 'dunces' after their leader's name, were very good at arguing for their point of view. When, after Scotus' death, new religious ideas reached Britain, his disciples refused to accept them. So at first the word 'dunce' meant someone who wouldn't accept new teachings. And when we call someone a dunce nowadays we should remember that John Duns Scotus, who wrote many books, was considered one of the cleverest men of his day!

Namby-Pamby is a curious expression that means 'weak' or 'soft'. The name comes from the nickname of a poet called **Ambrose Philips** (1674–1749). Philips got the name because of the rather weak and soppy poetry he wrote. As a poet, then, Philips was not very good and his best claim to fame was a lifelong quarrel with the great poet Alexander Pope (1688–1744), and of course the new word he gave to the English language!

If one side wins a **pyrrhic** victory it means that the victory was made at a great and damaging cost. **Pyrrhus** was the king of Epirus (319–272 BC) in Greece. A great soldier, Pyrrhus fought many battles against the Romans, often successfully. But after one battle Pyrrhus, who won but also lost many of his men, said, *'One more victory like that and we are lost.'* He was killed fighting the Romans.

Draconian means 'harsh' or 'cruel' and originated from **Draco**, a law maker in Athens, whose laws were very harsh.

A **Luddite** is a person who opposes modern technology and the word comes from the name of **Ned Lud**, who destroyed new machines in the eighteenth century.

Ritzy means 'fashionable, luxurious' and comes from **Cesar Ritz** (1850–1918), a Swiss who gave his name to the stylish Ritz hotels.

ROYAL PROGRESS

The English Royal Family stretches back many years. Did you know, for example, that Queen Elizabeth II is directly related to William the Conqueror? Even before William there were kings from different parts of the country who are distant relatives of the present monarchy.

Not all English rulers were called by the name we see in the history books – Henry V was often known as 'Hal' or 'Harry', Henry VIII was too. And although Henry VIII was obviously the 'eighth' Henry to be king, he was the first English monarch to give himself a number. Nor was Edward I the first 'Edward' to be king of England – for example there was Edward the Confessor who was king from 1042–1066.

If you're one of the many people who gets a little confused about just who was related to whom and how in the monarchy, then here's a little list to make everything clear. This royal line takes you from Elizabeth II right back to William the Conqueror, showing you how each monarch was related to the previous one:

Queen Elizabeth II is the daughter of. . . . . . .
George VI, who was the son of. . . . . . .

Edward VIII, who was the son of. . . . .
George V, who was the son of. . . . . .
Edward VII, who was the son of. . . . .
Queen Victoria, who was the niece of. . . . .
William IV, who was the brother of. . . . . .
George IV, who was the son of. . . .
George III, who was the grandson of . . .
George II, who was the son of. . . .
George I, who was the cousin of. . . .
Queen Anne, who was the sister-in-law of . . .
William III, who was the son-in-law of. . . .
James II, who was the brother of. . . .
Charles II, who was the son of . . .
Charles I, who was the son of. . . . .
James I, who was the cousin of. . . .
Elizabeth I, who was the half-sister of . . .
Mary I, who was the half-sister of. . . .
Edward VI, who was the son of. . . .
Henry VIII, who was the son of. . . .
Henry VII, who was the cousin of. . . .
Richard III, who was the uncle of. . . . .
Edward V, who was the son of. . . .
Edward IV, who was the cousin of. . . .
Henry VI, who was the son of. . . . .
Henry V, who was the son of. . . . .
Henry IV, who was the cousin of. . . .
Richard II, who was the grandson of. . . .
Edward III, who was the son of. . . . . .
Edward II, who was the son of. . . .
Edward I, who was the son of. . . . .
Henry III, who was the son of. . . .
John, who was the brother of. . . . . .
Richard I, who was the son of. . . .
Henry II, who was the cousin of. . . . .
Stephen, who was the cousin of. . . . .
Henry I, who was the brother of. . . .
William II, who was the son of. . . . .
William I. . . . . .

Is that clear?

Mnemonics

Schoolchildren are quite often tested on the names of kings and queens. There are a lot of different names to remember, but one way to make life a bit easier is by using a 'mnemonic'. These are words or phrases that help you to remember things better. The following mnemonic will help you remember those kings and queens:

Willie, Willie, Harry, Steve,
Harry, Dick, John, Harry Three,
One, Two, Three Neds, Richard Two,
Harry Four, Five, Six. Then who?
Edward Four, Five, Dick the Bad,
Harrys twain and Ned the Lad,
Mary, Bessie, James the Vain,
Charlie, Charlie, James again,
William and Mary, Anna Gloria,
Four Georges, William, and Victoria,
Edward Seventh next, and then
George the Fifth in 1910.
Edward the Eighth soon abdicated
And so a George was reinstated.

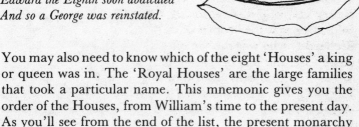

You may also need to know which of the eight 'Houses' a king or queen was in. The 'Royal Houses' are the large families that took a particular name. This mnemonic gives you the order of the Houses, from William's time to the present day. As you'll see from the end of the list, the present monarchy are members of the Windsor House.

The mnemonic is:

No Plan Like Yours To Study History Wisely.

Each first letter gives you the inital of one of the Houses, which in order are:

Norman
Plantagenet
Lancaster
York
Tudor
Stuart
Hanover
Windsor

SECRET MEANINGS

When we give a name to a baby we may be shaping its life more than we think. For thousands of years people have been looking for the 'secret meanings' of their names. One way of doing this is with numbers. If you think about it you'll realise that numbers are very important to us, for example, the number of our house, our telephone number, our date of birth and so on. Sometimes one particular number keeps repeating itself in your life. Of course this could just be an accident . . . but maybe it's your lucky number? The Greek mathematician Pythagoras was one of the first people to consider if numbers had a hidden meaning in our lives. Here is a simple way of finding the secret numbers that lie behind our names. One problem is that you can discover that your 'secret number' is not a very good one. Some people have even gone so far as to change their names to give themselves a better number!

Finding the Secret Number

The first step is to find the number: then this number can be checked to see what it means. We begin by giving each letter of the alphabet a number up to the value of nine. Obviously there are more than nine letters, so each number is given to more than one letter as this table shows:

1	2	3	4	5	6	7	8	9
A	B	C	D	E	F	G	H	I
J	K	L	M	N	O	P	Q	R
S	T	U	V	W	X	Y	Z	

Now that each letter has a number we can begin to add the letters in our name together to reach a number. In fact in this system we get three numbers: one from adding any vowels together – **a e i o u**, one from adding the consonants together – all the other letters of the alphabet, and the third by adding those two numbers together. We're now ready to see how this works on a real name. Remember, if the numbers add up to a number over nine then the digits of the number must be added together to make a number below nine. Here's an example: if a name adds up to 43, as this is over nine simply add them together 4 + 3 to get 7! If the number had been 49, then after adding 4 + 9 you'd get 13, still too much. So you then add 1 + 3 to get 4. Got it? Let's have a look at the numbers in the name of the famous English scientist Sir Isaac Newton.

```
vowels       9  + 1 + 1   +   5   +   6    = 21 = 2 + 1 = 3
             I  SA  AC  N  EW  TON
consonants   1   +   3 + 5 + 5 + 2 + 5 = 21 = 2 + 1 = 3
```

Total name: 3 + 3 = 6

So Newton's full reading is 3 – 3 – 6 Let's find out what it means.

The Number's Meaning

In general, **even** numbers are thought to be masculine and **odd** numbers are thought to be feminine in nature. But don't forget that it's not really a bad thing for a man to have a 'feminine' side to his character as well as a masculine one; indeed, most men and women have this natural balance. So there's no need for Newton to worry about having two odd numbers. Next we can see what each individual number means. This is done by using a special table made by **numerologists** – numerology is the long word for what we are doing now, finding out things by using numbers. Each number is given its own meaning.

1 **independent, ambitious**
2 **gentle, feminine, receptive**
3 **optimistic, artistic, brilliant**
4 **practical, steady, lacking ideas**
5 **eccentric, victorious, unstable**
6 **home-loving, simple**
7 **knowledgeable, lonely**
8 **rich, co-operative, powerful**
9 **idealistic, healthy**

In this system, Newton's **first number**, 3, from the vowels, is to do with a person's **hidden, private nature**. So from the table we can see that there is optimism and great ability in Newton. The **second number**, from the consonants, refers to a person's **outside or public life**. Here Newton also has ability and optimism – well, after all he was a great scientist! The **third number** tells us about the **complete person**. Interestingly, Newton's number, 6, shows him as a home-loving, simple-living person. This may seen odd for such a famous and brilliant man, but in fact Newton regarded himself as quite an ordinary person in many ways. So the numbers may be right after all!

Once you have worked out how to use the system as above you can start to use different tables, for instance one that links the numbers with colours:

1	black	6	grey
2	yellow	7	purple
3	white	8	brown
4	blue	9	red
5	green		

Or you could try a table that relates the numbers to days of the week:

1	Saturday, Wednesday	6	Monday, Friday
2	Sunday	7	Thursday
3	Thursday	8	Friday
4	Monday	9	Monday
5	Tuesday		

One more idea is to find the secret number hidden in your date of birth. So if you were born on the 20th of July 1962, for example, the sum would look like this: $2 + 0 + 7 + 1 + 9 + 6 + 2 = 27; 2 + 7 = 9$.

Using the System

Now you know how to find the numbers and what they mean you can start to use the system in all sorts of ways. A good place to start is on your own name, but be sure to use your name as it was written when you were first named – it may have changed since then. You can also use nicknames to find their secret meanings. Once you've got the hang of it you'll be able to find out what sort of characters your friends and family really are!

There are some interesting tests you could do. Some names can be spelt in more than one way, eg Geoffrey/Jeffrey and Claire/Clare. With the numbers system you can discover if the different spellings make any difference to the type of person. Let's have a look at these examples.

$$G + E + O + F + F + R + E + Y$$
$$7 + 5 + 6 + 6 + 6 + 9 + 5 + 7 = 15 = 5 + 1 = 6$$

$$J + E + F + F + R + E + Y$$
$$1 + 5 + 6 + 6 + 9 + 5 + 7 = 39 = 3 + 9 = 12 = 1 + 2 = 3$$

It seems that Jeffrey will be more artistic and brilliant than Geoffrey, who will be more of a home-lover.

$$C + L + A + I + R + E$$
$$3 + 3 + 1 + 9 + 9 + 5 = 30 = 3 + 0 = 3$$

$$C + L + A + R + E$$
$$3 + 3 + 1 + 9 + 5 = 21 = 2 + 1 = 3$$

So here at least it doesn't matter which spelling is used – Claire and Clare both have the same secret meaning. You can test some names for yourself – here are a few ideas:

Giles : Gyles
Anne : Ann
Stewart : Stuart
Brian : Bryan
Lyn : Lynne

This way of finding the secret numbers and meanings of our names is not the only one. The Druids had their own methods, and there is also a Hebrew system. But this is the simplest way to do it. Even if you don't believe that it works, numerology can be great fun if you share the 'secrets' among your friends. And who knows, you may find that your own secret number keeps cropping up more often in future!

TERRY AND TERESA, THOMAS AND THOMASINA

Our first names are very important to us: with a few exceptions they stay with us all our lives. Yet how many parents think about the meaning of the name they give to a child? Often names are chosen because they sound nice or because a particular name runs in the family. But all names meant something when they were first used, though nowadays these meanings have mostly been forgotten. In this look at name-meanings we shall rediscover the secrets behind some well-known first names. Who knows, if your parents had read this before you were born they might have named you differently . . .

Terry is now accepted as the short form of **Terence**. This was a Roman clan or family name, which may have come from the Latin *terere*, 'to rub'. Terence is quite a new name to England, though it was used in Ireland instead of the older *Turlough*. Once, however, it seems

Terry was a name on its own as a different form of **Derek**.

> **Teresa** comes from the Greek, and either means 'reaper', that is, someone who gathers, or possibly 'a woman from Therasia', which are two islands off the Greek coast. Until the 1500s Teresa seems to have been used only in Spain until the famous St Teresa of Avilon (1515–1582) made the name more popular. Some of the short names that have come from Teresa include **Tess**, **Tessie**, **Tracy** and **Terry**, names now used on their own.

Thomas is an old name that comes from Aramaic, the language that Jesus spoke. The name means 'twin,' and an early and famous Thomas was 'Doubting Thomas', one of Jesus's disciples, and the man who at first 'doubted' that Jesus had risen from the dead.

> **Thomasina** or **Thomasin** are girls' names that come from Thomas (see above). You'll probably know some of the other names for girls that come from this, like **Tamsin**, **Tammy** and **Tammie**.

John must be one of the most popular first names around. It has a very important history, and coming from the Hebrew, it means 'the Lord is gracious'. The name was made popular by John the Baptist and St John of the New Testament and by the twelfth century had come to Britain. We had a King John, of course, but one of the most well-loved 'Johns' was Robin Hood's giant friend Little John. In Ireland the name **Sean** is often used instead of John, and in

Wales another form, **Sion**, is sometimes heard. Nowadays babies are given the name **Jack** at birth but this name, like **Johnny** and **Jacky**, started as a short form of John.

Jane is a form of the name John, and so comes from the Hebrew **Johanna**. Although it is one of the popular girls' names now, Jane was hardly ever used in Britain until the 1500s. One of the six wives of Henry VIII was called Jane – Jane Seymour, who died after giving birth to the future king Edward VI. Many other girls' names came from the same beginning as Jane, for instance **Jean**, **Joanna**, **Jenny**, **Janet** and **Sheena**.

Geoffrey seems to have come from the old word *Gaufrid*, a name meaning 'district', though it is similar to the old word *Godafrid*, meaning 'god-peace', from which **Godfrey** comes. Wherever they came from, Geoffrey, or Jeffrey as it is often spelt, is now a lot more common than Godfrey. One of the earliest and best known Geoffreys was the writer Geoffrey Chaucer, who wrote his *Canterbury Tales* in the fourteenth century.

Jennifer is a name with a noble past. It is a Cornish name which comes from **Guenevere**, who was the wife of King Arthur. Guenevere, or **Guinevere**, seems to have meant 'fair' or, some think, 'white-faced'. The unusual names **Ganor**, **Ginevra** and **Vanora** all come from Guenevere.

Susan is a pretty name with a pretty beginning. There was a city in Persia (now Iran) called Shushan which was often spoken of in the Bible. This was the City of White Lilies, and in Hebrew *shushannah* means 'lily'. From this came the longer form of the name, Susanna, which was how the name was usually spelt until Susan became popular with the Victorians. We can easily see that **Sue** and **Susie** are short forms but in the eighteenth or nineteenth centuries **Suke** or **Suky** may have been more common.

George is a popular name and six kings of England have borne it, as well as important figures like George Washington, first President of the United States. The name comes from the Greek *georgos* which means 'tiller of the soil' or 'farmer'.

It can be fun to look around at your friends and see what their names mean and whether they seem 'true' of them. For example, someone called **Hilary** should be 'cheerful', while **Gemma** may well be a 'gem' of a girl. If you're fortunate enough to be called **Matthew** then you are a 'gift of Jehovah (God)', but if you go by the name of **Wayne** you could be a lowly 'wagon maker'. The delightful **Melissa** could be as 'busy as a bee', though **Bernard** is more likely to show himself as 'brave as a bear' while **Philip**, if he's true to his Greek origins, will be a 'lover of horses'. Lucky **Estelle** is a real 'star', and from the 'grand hill' where **Gordon** might live you may be able to see the house of **Clive**, who is a 'dweller by the cliff'.

This will give you some idea of the fun you can have with first names and their meanings. Look through this list and see if you can find your name and the names of your friends:

Girls

Alice – 'nobility'
Amanda – 'lovable'
Angela – 'messenger'
Ann – 'God has favoured me'
Audrey – 'noble strength'
Bianca – 'white'
Brenda – 'sword'
Cara – 'dear one'
Catherine – 'pure'
Claire – 'bright, clear'
Donna – 'lady'
Dorothy – 'gift of God'
Emma – 'whole, universal'
Eve – 'lively'
Felicity – 'happiness'
Helen – 'the bright one'
Jessica – 'God beholds'
Leah – 'cow'
Leigh – 'meadow'
Margaret – 'pearl'
Mary – 'wished-for child'
Melanie – 'black'
Nadine – 'hope'
Natalie – 'Christmas Day'
Rebecca – 'a snare'
Renee – 're-born'
Sara – 'princess'
Serena – 'serene'
Sophia – 'wisdom'

Sylvia – 'wood'
Verity – 'truth'
Zoe – 'life'

Boys

Alexander – 'defending men'
Andrew – 'manly'
Charles – 'a man'
Donald – 'world mighty'
Edward – 'happy guardian'
Francis – 'freedom'
Gareth – 'old man'
Harvey – 'battle worthy'
Lance – 'land'
Neil – 'champion'
Patrick – 'a nobleman'
Peter – 'stone'
Richard – 'stern ruler'
Robert – 'bright fame'
Samuel – 'name of God'
Stephen – 'crown'
Trevor – 'big village'
Victor – 'conqueror'
Vincent – 'conquering'
Zachary – 'Jehovah has remembered'

UNDERWOOD AND WODEHOUSE·

Whenever you have to fill in a form or put your name in a register the most important part of your name is the surname, and if you give your name to someone you usually tell them your surname first. Yet it was only in the eleventh century AD that people had surnames at all. Before that people might have had two names but they weren't passed on through the family in the way that our names are.

Where did these names come from? All surnames meant something once, so let's find out where some common family names sprang from, and what they mean . . .

A couple of common surnames these days are **Underwood** and **Wodehouse** or **Woodhouse**. Both of them stem from the same 'root' word which, as you can see, is **Wood**. Like many surnames Wood got its name from a natural feature. Trees and woods were once much more widespread than they are now. Someone called **'ate Wood'** would have lived 'at the wood', and many people took this name. **Underwood** would have described where a person lived – in this case perhaps at the bottom of a wooded hill.

But **Wodehouse** was not a name given to someone living in a wooden house . . . for in the days when surnames first came to be used nearly everyone lived in such a dwelling! It would have meant a house that was in a wood. Lots of different names come from **Wood** – **Blackwood**, **Woodman** and **Attwood** are just three examples.

If you're one of the 107,000 or so people in Britain with the surname **Bailey** you'll be pleased to know that your ancestors were quite important people. The name comes from *baillif* and *baillis*, Old French for bailiff. Bailiffs were officials who used to collect money or help run estates. The name Bailey came to England in 1066 with William the Conqueror. Other names that come from the same root are **Bayle**, **Baylies** and **Bayliss**.

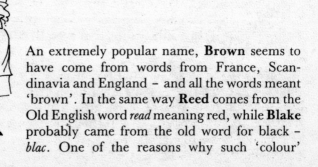

An extremely popular name, **Brown** seems to have come from words from France, Scandinavia and England – and all the words meant 'brown'. In the same way **Reed** comes from the Old English word *read* meaning red, while **Blake** probably came from the old word for black – *blac*. One of the reasons why such 'colour'

names were so common, perhaps, is that at the time when surnames came into being Britain was full of people from different tribes and countries. This meant that the differences in hair and colouring would have been greater than is usual today and so worth making note of – possibly with a name.

A suitable job for anyone with the surname **Clark** would be as a clergyman or simply a clerk. In the Middle Ages when most people couldn't read or write, most of the secretarial work was done by churchmen – 'clerics'. Clark or **Clarke** was the surname that grew out of this, and was given to people who were able to do what we would now call office work. Although Clarke is the most popular of the names from this source, folk with the name **Clerk** are nearer the original Latin word, *clericus*.

Lucky people have the name **Edwards**. The original Old English word from which it comes, *Eadweard*, meant 'guardian of happiness' and both the surname and the first name come from this source. Edwards is often considered to be a typically English name, and it was very popular as a first name in this country long before William the Conqueror ever reached these shores. There are nearly 180,000 people with this surname in Britain. Other forms of it are **Edkins**, **Edwardson** and even **Beddard**.

Anyone with the surname **Hall** who lives in a big house is being true to their origins. An Old English word, *Heall* meant a hall or large house, and the first Halls must have either lived in the local manor house or worked in or near it. The discoverer of Halley's Comet, **Edward Halley**

(1656–1742) has a surname that would have come from the same root as Hall – as did **Hailey**, **Hallam**, **Halstone** and **Halman**.

Kelly is a very common Irish surname which has spread all over the world. *O'Ceallaigh* is the Gaelic word which gave rise to the surname, but no one is sure what this means. However, *ceallach* is the Gaelic word for 'fight' or 'battle' so the name could have been given to those men who were brave in battle. As Kelly is the second most common surname in Ireland this means there must have been a lot of mighty warriors in that land!

People with the name **Lewis** certainly were warrior-like for Lewis began as a forename meaning 'celebrated in battle'. This name has had a lengthy trip around Europe, taking on the form of **Ludwig** in Germany, where it began, going to France as **Louis**, and to Italy as **Luigi**. Some think that many Welsh people with the surname Lewis took it as an 'English' version of Llewelyn in the Middle Ages. Also, quite recently, Europeans who have come to England with names such as **Levinsky** have changed them to Lewis. All of this helps explain why there are as many as 180,000 Lewises in the British Isles.

Parker came to England after 1066, and takes its meaning from the Old French word *parquer*, meaning park keeper. These parks, however, would have been rather different from the quiet, well-kept areas we now have. People called **Park** or **Parkes** may have lived or worked in parks. **Parkman**, **Parkhouse** and the French **Duparc** ('of the park') all come from this root.

> Should you rejoice in the name of **Smith**, then you are one of about 800,000 people in Britain with the surname – in America there are well over two million! This name is a very old one and comes from the Old English *smith* which meant 'metal worker'. **Goldsmith** and **Black-smith** are two obvious examples of names coming from Smith. But do you recognise **Schmidt** (Germany), **Lefevre** (France), **Kovac** (Slavonic), **Haddad** (Hebrew) or **Faber** (Latin)? These are the different forms that Smith has taken as the name travels around.

Wilson has the same root as **Williams** and comes from the word *willahelm*, which meant 'a willing man with a helmet'! **William** became very popular as a first name, but by the fourteenth century Wilson had become widely used as a surname.

The Celts of Scotland and the west of Britain have left a number of surnames which, as you'll see from this list, are very widespread nowadays.

Bevan – son of Evan
Burns – dweller by the stream
Duncan – brown warrior
Lloyd – grey

McPherson – son of the parson
Murphy – descendant of the 'sea warrior'
Stewart – steward
Trevean – dweller in the little homestead
Vaughan – the little man

.If you haven't come across your own name yet you may find it
in this last list. Remember, lots of names come from the same
original word so it's worth looking under names that sound or
look similar to your own.

Baker – a baker
Bennett – blessed
Campbell – wry/crooked mouth
Cooper – maker of barrels/buckets
Docherty – stern, hurtful
Fuller – someone who finished cloth
Green – village green
Hughes – dependant of Hugh
Jones – dependant of John
Lee – wood/clearing/pasture
McKay – son of Aodh, 'fire'
Miller – grinder of corn
Patterson – son of Patrick, 'nobleman'
Reilly – descendant from Raghallach – 'the valiant one'
Ross – fame; also, 'from a heath'
Scott – person from Scotland
Taylor – a tailor
Turner – someone who used a lathe
Ward – one who keeps watch
Webster – a weaver
Wright – a carpenter

VERA RAVE

Who is Vera Rave? The answer is she's probably a friend of
Miles Smile and Marcel Calmer – for in each of their names
the surname is an anagram of the first name. An anagram is a
word that can be made by changing around the letters of
another word, like **medal** and **lamed**, or **tough** and **ought**. A
surprising number of names make anagrams, including the
names of some very famous people. Here are five presidents
of the United States:

Grover Cleveland – Govern, clever lad!
Theodore Roosevelt – Hero told to oversee
President Franklin Delano Roosevelt – Lo!
real keen person voted first in land
Dwight D. Eisenhower – Wow! he's right
indeed!
Ronald Reagan – An oral danger

Other well-known people who make interesting anagrams
include:

Adolf Hitler – Hated for ill

Florence Nightingale – Flit on, cheering angel

Disraeli (Prime Minister) – I lead, sir
Alexander the Great – General taxed earth
Thomas Alva Edison, (the inventor) – He lit
homes, and over vast nation
Saint George and the Dragon – Ha! a strong
giant ended ogre

You'll find some more famous people in the lists below.

Kant : tank
Lenin : linen
Luther : hurtle
Socrates : coasters
Rasputin : puritans
Darwin : inward

Canute : uncate
Peron : prone
Castro : actors
Pasteur : pasture
Einstein : nineties
Edison : onside

By now you may be wondering if your name can make an
anagram. Have a look at these two lists, one of boys' and one

of girls' names, and see. If your name is not listed, try and make one up yourself.

Boys

Alec : lace
Neil : line
Liam : mail
Ezra : raze
Evan : vane
Kurt : turk
Lewis : wiles
Denis : snide
Craig : cigar
Brian : brain
Cyril : lyric
Claud : ducal
Edwin : widen
Edgar : grade
Alvin : anvil
Piers : spire
Silas : sails

Pedro : roped
Alban : banal
Gerard : grader
Gerald : glared
Steven : events
Dorian : ordain
Ernest : enters
Dennis : sinned
Alfred : flared
Osbert : sorbet
Andrew : wander
Stefan : fasten
Simeon : movies
Adrian : radian
Rodney : yonder
Samson : masons
Daniel : nailed

Girls

May (or **Amy**) : yam
Meg : gem
Tess : sets
Kate : teak
Olga : goal
Edna : dean
Lisa : sail
Rose : sore
Lena : lean
Enid : dine
Lydia : daily
Freda : fared

Mary : army
Clea : lace
Lois : soil
Rosa : soar
Susie : issue
Cathy : yacht
Rosie : osier
Greta : great
Esther : threes
Bertha : breath
Teresa : Easter
Thelma : Hamlet

Tessa : asset	**Ingrid** : riding
Sadie : ideas	**Astril** : trails
Mabel : amble/blame	**Glynis** : singly
Bella : label	**Martina** : Martian
Cilla : lilac	**Melissa** : aimless
Delia : ideal	**Deirdre** : redried
Laura : aural	**Sallie** : allies
Rhoda : hoard	**Isabella** : sailable

WELLINGTON'S BOOTS

If you were a gentleman in the nineteenth century you couldn't be without a pair and, if you're out in the rain these days, they are equally important: Wellington boots. They are the most famous boots in history, and their name comes, of course, from the **Duke of Wellington** (1769–1852). This great man made the wearing of knee-length boots very popular, especially when he wore them at the Battle of Waterloo in 1815. In those days the boots were made out of leather instead of rubber and were cut away behind the knee.

'Wellies' are not the only fashion or invention to take their name from a real person. Some very familiar everyday objects have gained their names from the person who invented them or first made them popular. This is the greatest honour an inventor can have . . . so let's salute a select band of brainy, brilliant – or perhaps just lucky – human beings.

One of the first sights any tourist in London visits is **Big Ben**, the popular name for the large bell and also the clock and tower of the Houses of Parliament. Yet while there is no doubt that Big Ben is an impressive sight and sound, not everyone agrees over how it got its name. Some say the bell was named after **Sir Benjamin Hall** (1802–1867) who was in charge of the building when the original bell was put there. Others claim that it was named after the popular boxer **Benjamin Caunt**, who at over 2 metres and 85 kilos was certainly a big Ben!

Many people don't realise that the **biro** was named after the pen's inventor, **Lazlo Biro**. Biro was a Hungarian who went to Argentina during the Second World War, taking with him his new ideas for a pen. It worked by having a little ball at the end of its nib – such pens are often called 'ball-points' – and was easier and cleaner to use than a normal ink pen. By 1944 the new 'biro' already had an important use. Allied pilots used these pens for writing, for unlike fountain pens it seems they do not leak at high altitudes!

Hoover, a common name for the vacuum cleaner, comes from an American, **William H. Hoover** (1849–1932), which is odd – for he didn't invent the machine! Hoover, a clever businessman, persuaded J. Murray Spangler, a caretaker from Ohio, to sell him the rights to a new cleaner Spangler had invented. In 1908 Hoover set up the Hoover Suction Sweeper Company, and by 1911 he was selling the machines in Britain. Although similar cleaners had been used here since 1900 the name Hoover soon became identified with all vacuum cleaners. But if only poor J. Murray Spangler had kept his invention people might now be 'spanglering' their carpets instead of 'hoovering' them!

Peach Melba, a dessert of peaches and ice-cream was named in honour of the Australian opera singer **Dame Nellie Melba** (1861–1931). Famous chef Escoffier invented this dessert when Dame Nellie wanted peaches for dessert at a party she was giving, and others thought ices would be better. The great chef compromised . . . and put the two together!

The **sandwich** has been around for hundreds of years but it was only in the eighteenth century that it gained its familiar name. The Fourth Earl of Sandwich, **John Montagu** (1718–1792), was a well-known gambler. On one occasion in 1762 he spent twenty-four hours at the card table. Overcome by hunger, but unwilling to leave his game, the Earl told his servant to fetch him a slice of beef between two slices of bread. This was the forerunner of the modern sandwich – though such snacks are nowadays seen more often at picnics than in gambling casinos!

If you keep your eyes open you'll probably be able to find some more inventions that have taken their names from real people. The following are a few more of the popular ones:

Belisha beacon	flashing light on pole at zebra crossing	Sir Leslie Hore-Belisha (1893–1957)
Braille	reading system for blind	Louis Braille (1809–1852)
Cardigan	knitted wool jacket	7th Earl of Cardigan, James Brudenell (1797–1868)
Mackintosh	waterproof coat	Charles Mackintosh (1766–1843)
Morse code	code for sending messages	Samuel Morse (1791–1872)
Saxophone	musical instrument	Antoine Sax (1814–1894)

XAVIER AND OTHER SAINTS

A saint is a holy person who has been honoured by the Church for something he or she has done – though the honour usually comes long after the person has died! There are thousands of people who have become saints and many of them led very interesting lives. An example of a modern person who may one day be a saint is **Mother Teresa of Calcutta**, who has devoted her life to helping the poor and sick.

Here we go back into history and consider some of the men and women who have reached the high status of saint.

St Francis Xavier was a missionary, which means he spent his time travelling and telling people about Christianity. Xavier journeyed all over India, Japan and Malaysia. He died in 1552 from a fever while waiting to travel into China to continue his work.

St Hilary was the Bishop of Poitiers in France in the fourth century. St Hilary's Day is January 13th, and at one time the Hilary term at Oxford University always began on this date after Christmas.

The third-century Roman priest **St Valentine** is always connected with love, because of St Valentine's Day on February 14th, but this happened only by accident. Valentinius, as the priest was called, was martyred on the day before the Roman festival of Juno. At this festival people would draw lots for the choice of lovers. This custom was carried on to the day we now call St Valentine's Day – even though the priest's only connection with it was to die the day before the feast!

Many legends surround **St Joseph of Arimathea**, the man who buried the body of Jesus after the crucifixion. Legend has it that Joseph brought the Holy Grail, the cup containing Jesus's blood from the cross, to Glastonbury in England. This was the cup sought by the Knights of King Arthur's Round Table. Joseph is also supposed to have planted his staff at Glastonbury – where it grew into a tree.

As all Englishmen should know, **St George**'s Day is on the 23rd of April – he is, after all, the patron saint of England. Very little is known about the real George, except that he was a Roman army officer known as 'The Great Martyr' for the brave way he died for his religion. His death was probably in AD 303 but, alas, the legend about him slaying the dragon is probably just folk-lore with little truth behind it. Saints were often shown in pictures and on badges fighting dragons, as these creatures represented evil.

St Swithin is a saint who makes the weather-man's job easy! For tradition has it that if it rains on July 15th, St Swithin's Day, then it will rain for the next 40 days! He was a man who hated unnecessary ceremony and tradition, but after his death his remains were unearthed and reburied in the much grander Winchester Cathedral. The prophecy is said to be St Swithin's revenge.

St Francis of Assisi is a popular and well-known saint, who gave up the life of a rich mer-chant's son to become a humble and poor priest. He is the patron saint of animals and is often pic-tured surrounded by birds and animals. He was born Giovanni Bernardone, and was only later called Francis because of the 'Frenchified' way he behaved as a young man.

The fourth-century saint **St Martin** showed his kindness one cold winter's night when he cut his military cloak in half to clothe a freezing beggar. He was a soldier who later became Bishop of Tours in France. Since 1918 his feast day, Mar-tinmas on November 11th, has been on the same day as Armistice Day, the anniversary of peace at the end of the First World War.

St Catherine of Alexandria, whose feast day is November 25th, was a beautiful woman of noble birth who met a horrible death. At a festival held by the emperor Maximillian, Catherine upset everyone, including the emperor, by saying she was a Christian and so couldn't continue with the non-Christian ceremony. Furious, the emperor had her stripped and tied to great wheels studded with nails that would rip her to pieces. Some say that the wheels broke and that she escaped to the mountains – where she was killed by soldiers! The firework we know as the Catherine Wheel is named after this brave woman.

Surely the most famous saint of all, **St Nicholas**, Santa Claus, is loved by children all over the world for the presents he brings at Christmas time. St Nicholas, whose feast day is in fact December 6th not Christmas Day, was Bishop of Myra in the fourth century. His reputation for giving gifts comes from the following story. Nicholas overheard a poor man saying that he

could not afford to marry off his daughters so he
would have to sell them. Nicholas is said to have
left three bags of gold at the poor man's house,
one for each of his three daughters.

There are many saints who are 'patron' saints, that is, they
are supposed to look after whatever they are patron of. Here is
a list of some of them and the things they 'patronise'.

St Agnes – engaged couples, gardeners
St Ambrose – bee-keepers, pets
St Andrew – Scotland, fishermen, sailors
St Anthony – lost things
St Augustine – theologians
St Barbara – builders, firework makers
St Boniface – brewers, tailors
St Cecilia – musicians
St Christopher – travellers, sailors
St David – Wales
St Dunstan – blacksmiths, goldsmiths, the blind
St Elizabeth – bakers, beggars
St Gabriel – postmen
St George – England, chivalry, soldiers
St Jerome – students
St Joseph – carpenters, engineers, family
St Jude – lost causes
St Margaret – women, nurses, peasants
St Matthew – bankers, tax-collectors
St Peter – butchers, bakers, clockmakers
St Theresa of Avila – those in need of grace
St Thomas – architects, carpenters
St Ursula – maidens, teachers
St Zita – domestic servants.

Y, FRANCE

If you were to write a postcard and address it *'Why France'* the postman would not be fooled. He'd know that it was intended for a little town in France that simply bears the name **Y**. Another single letter town is **E** in the United States. Sweden and Denmark and Japan each have an **O**, and the Caroline Islands boast a little place called **U**!

From **Aachen** (West Germany) to **Zzwiec** (Poland), the world is full of zany names. If people chose their holiday places by names rather than by sun and sand, then Majorca and Palma would be pushed out of the holiday brochures by **Tumucumaque** (Brazil), **Kurri Kurri** (New South Wales, Australia) and **Zaranda** (Nigeria)!

How Far to Faaa?

Travel far enough North and you come to Hell . . . or at least, you come to the town of **Hell** in Norway. There's also a **Hel** in Poland. A few place-names make you look twice to see if the spelling's correct – can there really be three As in **Faaa** – a town in Tahiti for example, or four in **Kaaawa**, a town near Hawaii? Equally odd is the place in Jordan called **Jijjih**, and also Nigeria's **Uburu-Uku**. But for unusual spelling it's hard to beat this place in Sweden – **Kvikkjokk**, which has five Ks!

Strange place-names can make you wonder how places came to be so called. Why is **Rabbit River** so called – do bunnies use the water to wash in? **Goodenough Island**, near New Zealand must have satisfied someone once, but how did **Overwinning** in South Africa get its name?

Doubtless not many people live in the town of **Lytle** in America, though there should be more in **Many**, but the biggest population should surely be in **Most** in Czechoslovakia. The settlement of **Bor** in the Sudan doesn't sound very exciting. Much more inviting is **Kissimme** in the United States – the locals must be very friendly! But if you're looking to travel somewhere to make a new start in life then look no further than a town in Canada – it's simply called **Success**.

US Eh!

Some of the oddest place-names belong to the United States.
All of the following are real places (with the state in which you
can find them):

Aaat's Bay – Alaska
Battiest – Oklahoma
Bug – Kentucky
Crooksville – Ohio
Ding Dong – Texas
Eek – Alaska
Embarrass – Wisconsin
Hi Hat – Kentucky
Hungry Horse – Montana
Marrowbone – Kentucky
Nameless – Kentucky
Social Circle – Georgia
Sweet Gum Head – Louisiana
Truth or Consequences – New Mexico
Uncle Same – Louisiana
Why – Arizona
Whynot – Mississippi
Zzyzx Springs – California

ZERO ZZYZZ

Most of us don't take much notice of our surnames. They become as familiar and as ordinary to us as an arm or a leg. But for a few people their surname can be a burden. These are the folk who only have to say their family name for it to raise a smile or a snigger. In this section we take a look at some of these remarkable names, though we begin with those who have actually chosen to have an odd surname.

In the United States great pride is taken in being the last person to appear in the telephone directory. So much so that individuals have accepted the cost of choosing silly names to become: **Zero Zzyzz** and **Vladimir Zzzyd** of Miami, **Zeke Zzzypt** of Chicago and the incredible **Zachary Zzzzzzzzzra** of San Francisco, whose surname has a remarkable nine Zs in it!

If you're a lazy person then nothing could be better than to have a surname that could be written in one letter. And in fact there are some such names. **U**, **E** and **O** are used in the world as surnames, while at various times these letters have been surnames in the United Kingdom: **A**, **B**, **J**, **N** and **O**. Almost as easy to write are the names **By**, **Ng**, **Ou**, **Oy** and **Za**.

Believe it or not there is a family in France which has the surname **1792**! As if this wasn't enough, some of the family have been given unusual first names – at one time four brothers in the family were called **January**, **February**, **March** and **April**!

Aaberg to Zysk

Names should be enjoyed. If you have an unusual surname don't try to hide it: be proud of it and be glad that you're different from all those Smiths and Joneses. For anyone who wants to choose an unusual or fun name here is a list of interesting possibilities . . . every one is a genuine surname!

Asparagus	Moron
Baba	Muckenfuss
Clutterbuck	Muddyman
Drinkdregs	Obedience
Earwig	Oliphant
Feeblebunny	Pancake
Fluke	Pfannbecker
Fullalove	Prettybody
Giggle	Quackenbush
Goon	Twaddle
Livengood	Von Garlic
Maggot	Whalebelly

124

THE BIG BOOK OF SUPERSTITIONS
by Gyles Brandreth; illustrated by Kate Shannon

Could this be your lucky day?

* If you meet a frog in the middle of the road, you will soon get some money.
* If you pull your finger joints and they make a cracking sound, you know somebody loves you.

But –

* If a bird dropping lands on your head – IT WILL BRING BAD LUCK!

Take your fate firmly in your hands – and read on!

0 552 542679

THE BIG BOOK OF SILLY QUESTIONS
by Gyles Brandreth; illustrated by John Carter

* If "Dr Livingston, I presume," was the answer, what was
  the question?
  "What is your full name, Dr Presume?"

* Which is bigger, Mrs Bigger or Mrs Bigger's baby?
  Mrs Bigger's baby is a little Bigger!

* Which is colder, –40°C or –40°F?
  They are both the same!

If you think these questions are silly – wait until you see the
rest of the book! And some of the ridiculous quizzes are not
as crazy as they may seem. . . .

0 552 542636

If you would like to receive a newsletter telling you about our new children's books, fill in the coupon with your name and address and send it to:

The Childrens Books Editor
Transworld Publishers Ltd.,
Century House,
61/63 Uxbridge Road, Ealing,
London, W5 5SA

Name ....

Address ....

....

....

CHILDREN'S NEWSLETTER